The Tomorrow's Job
Thriving in a World of Change
M. Hijazi

Table of Content

Author's Words 5
Introduction: The Changing Landscape of Jobs 7
Chapter 1: What is a Job? 11
Chapter 2: Types of Jobs 17
Chapter 3: Evolution of Job Functions 25
Chapter 4: Job Trends from the 1970s to the 1990s 33
Chapter 5: The Dot-Com Boom and Globalization (1990s to Early 2000s) 39
Chapter 6: Most Wanted Skills in the Modern Job Market 46
Chapter 7: Current Job Offers and High-Demand Roles 54
Chapter 8: The Impact of AI and Automation on Today's Workforce 63
Chapter 9: The Role of Imagination and Creativity in Future Jobs .. 71
Chapter 10: The Decline of Specialized Skills and the Future of Broad-Based Knowledge 79
Chapter 11: The Future of Entrepreneurship and Self-Employment 87
Chapter 12: The Future of Jobs in Emerging Technologies 96
Chapter 13: The Most Promising Industries of the Future 105
Chapter 14: The Future of Work – Embracing Change and Opportunity 114
Chapter 15: What to Learn for Jobs in the Next 5 Years 122
Chapter 16: Preparing for Jobs in the Next 10 Years 128
Chapter 17: Practical Tips for Staying Ahead 134
Chapter 18: The 50 Most Wanted Jobs of the Future 137

Expanded List of Jobs with References and Logic 139
Chapter 19: AI Specialist 158
Chapter 20: Cybersecurity Analyst 162
Chapter 21: Biotechnology Engineer 166
Chapter 22: Renewable Energy Technician 170
Chapter 23: Quantum Computing Scientist 174
Chapter 24: Preparing for Future Jobs – Practical Tips and Advice 178
Chapter 25: Preparing for Specific Future Jobs (Based on the Top 50) 184
Chapter 26: Embracing the Future with Confidence........188

Author's Words

As a business consultant with over 22 years of experience, working across various industries and countries, I've had the opportunity to see firsthand what it takes to succeed in today's ever-changing world. And what I've learned can be distilled into a few key principles.

First, **we are working to live, not living to work**. Our careers should support our lives, not consume them. We work to provide, to grow, and to experience life, never forget that balance.

In business, **numbers tell us the truth**, but only when they come from the right source and are correctly understood. Don't be misled by false data or manipulated facts. Learn to see through the noise and recognize that **reality is always the key to success**. Leave behind illusions and focus on what's real, what you can control, and what genuinely matters.

It's true that **life is not fair**, and it never will be. But that doesn't mean we need to become ruthless or cold-hearted. Instead, we need to be **trained and disciplined**, ready to face life's challenges with resilience and intelligence. The real power isn't in your hands or in brute strength, it's in your mind. **Develop your mind, enhance your intelligence**, and you'll find that the world opens up to you. Today, with the vast amount of information and knowledge available at your fingertips, you have everything you need to be the best version of yourself.

Don't let fear control you. **Being afraid is never the solution**. Mistakes will happen, and when they do, embrace them. **Mistakes are your greatest teachers**, they shape you, refine you, and ultimately make you better. So don't give up when you stumble. Keep pushing forward, knowing that each misstep is part of the journey toward success.

And most importantly, remember this: **the future belongs to those who are willing to adapt and learn**. The world is full of opportunities, and your success lies in your ability to seize them. Intelligence, creativity, and adaptability are your most powerful tools. **You have the power to shape your future**, all it takes is a willingness to grow and a belief in your ability to thrive.

Introduction: The Changing Landscape of Jobs

In recent years, many people have started to worry about the future of jobs. It seems like every day, we hear concerns about how technology, automation, and artificial intelligence (AI) are changing the world so fast that people are afraid they won't be able to keep up. The fear is that future jobs will require complex skills in areas like software development, digital marketing, web design, and a deep understanding of technical systems. Some feel that if they don't possess these highly specialized skills, they won't stand a chance in the workforce of tomorrow.

However, I believe this fear is misplaced. The truth is, the future of jobs will not be about mastering every technical detail or keeping up with the latest software updates. Instead, the most valuable skill will be the ability to think creatively, imagine new possibilities, and come up with innovative ideas. This shift is happening right before our eyes. In a world where technology can do so much for us, the real demand will be for people who can guide that technology with fresh ideas and a different way of thinking.

Why You Shouldn't Be Afraid of AI

Many people see AI as a threat, an advanced force that will take away jobs or make human workers obsolete. But this perspective overlooks the incredible potential of AI as a tool. AI isn't here to replace us; it's here to make our lives easier, and in many cases, to help us bring our ideas to life faster than we could on our own. Tasks that used to take years of study and experience, such as website development, graphic design, music production, and even complex financial modeling, can now be done in minutes with the help of AI tools.

For example, imagine you want to start a new business but don't know where to begin. In the past, you would have had to spend weeks or even months learning about business strategies, customer demographics, financial planning, and market trends. Today, with AI, you can ask for a detailed business plan in a matter of minutes. It's not just about the information AI can provide, it's about how quickly and efficiently it allows you to act on your ideas.

And that's the key difference. Future jobs will belong to those who have the imagination and creativity to use these tools effectively. If you have an idea, AI can help you make it a reality without needing to learn all the technical skills yourself.

Who Should Really Be Worried?

Interestingly, it's not everyday people who should be concerned about the future, it's professionals who have spent years mastering specific, technical skills. Jobs that require highly specialized knowledge, such as IT engineers, doctors, or accountants, may be the most at risk. AI is getting so advanced that it can now do many of the tasks these professionals perform, from diagnosing illnesses to optimizing network systems.

For example, AI-powered diagnostic tools are already being used in medicine to read x-rays, analyze lab results, and even suggest treatment plans. Similarly, in IT, AI systems can manage complex networks, detect security threats, and automate routine maintenance tasks, things that previously required a team of engineers. The professions we have traditionally thought of as "safe" may be the ones that undergo the biggest changes as AI continues to evolve.

This doesn't mean these jobs will disappear entirely, but they will change. Instead of being the experts who execute complex tasks, these professionals may need to focus on higher-level strategic thinking, guiding the systems that now handle the technical details.

What the Future Really Needs: Creative Thinkers

So, if the future isn't about specialized skills, what will it be about? The answer lies in imagination and creativity. The future job market will reward those who can think differently, generate new ideas, and find innovative ways to apply technology. The ability to solve problems, connect with people, and come up with original concepts will be far more valuable than any technical skill set.

This is why there's no need to fear the future if you don't know how to code, design a website, or manage complex systems. As long as you have ideas and the ability to think creatively, you'll be well-prepared for the jobs of tomorrow.

The following chapters will explore the evolution of jobs, the skills in demand today, and what we can expect in the future. But remember this: the future belongs to those who can think creatively and use technology as a tool, not to those who fear it.

Chapter 1: What is a Job?

Jobs have always played a vital role in human societies, providing both economic stability and personal fulfillment. The concept of a job has evolved over time, reflecting changes in societal structures, economic systems, and technological advancements. In its simplest form, a job can be defined as any activity or task performed by an individual in exchange for payment (Smith, 2019). However, this definition only scratches the surface of what jobs have meant historically and what they mean today.

Early Concepts of Work and Survival

In ancient times, the concept of a job was tied directly to survival. People worked to provide the basic necessities, food, shelter, and security, for themselves and their families. Work was often communal, with early human societies relying on hunting, gathering, and farming. Every member of the community contributed in some way, whether by gathering food, caring for children, or building shelters. These tasks were not considered "jobs" in the modern sense, but they were essential roles within the community (Jones & Turner, 2020).

As societies developed and grew more complex, so did the concept of work. Specialization became necessary as people took on different roles to support the community. Some individuals became skilled hunters, while others became craftsmen, farmers, or traders. This specialization marked the early development of what we now think of as professions. Over time, these specialized roles became formalized, with people being recognized for their expertise in particular areas (Garrett, 2018).

The Emergence of Professions

As cities and civilizations expanded, job roles became more diverse and specialized. The rise of trade and commerce during the ancient and medieval periods created new professions, such as merchants, artisans, and scribes. These early professionals were often highly regarded in society due to the specialized nature of their skills and knowledge. Professions like blacksmithing, pottery, and weaving, which required years of training and apprenticeship, were central to the economies of early civilizations (Garrett, 2018).

During this time, the concept of work began to move beyond mere survival. Jobs started to serve a dual purpose: they provided individuals with a livelihood and helped establish their social standing. A person's job became a key part of their identity, shaping their role within the community (Williams, 2021). This trend has continued into modern times, with many people defining themselves by their occupation, from farmers and teachers to doctors and engineers.

Jobs in the Industrial Revolution

The Industrial Revolution, which began in the late 18th century, marked one of the most significant shifts in the concept of work. For the first time, large numbers of people left agricultural work and rural settings to take up jobs in factories in rapidly growing cities (Mokyr, 2002). The rise of mechanized production meant that jobs could now be done faster and more efficiently, but it also led to the creation of new job roles, such as machine operators, factory overseers, and industrial managers.

The nature of work during the Industrial Revolution was radically different from what had come before. Whereas most work in the pre-industrial world was centered around the home or small workshops, industrial jobs were located in massive factories, often requiring long hours and repetitive tasks (Baldwin, 2019). Workers became part of a larger system of production, contributing to the mass manufacture of goods that were sold both domestically and internationally.

For the first time, the idea of working for wages became the norm for a significant portion of the population. People traded their time and labor for money, which they then used to support themselves and their families. This development laid the foundation for the modern job market, where individuals sell their labor to employers in exchange for wages or salaries.

Modern-Day Jobs: A Shift Towards Knowledge and Technology

In the 20th and 21st centuries, the job market underwent another transformation, this time driven by technology and the rise of the knowledge economy. As countries industrialized and technological advances accelerated, manual labor began to decline in importance, while jobs that required intellectual and creative skills became more valued (Friedman, 2005). The knowledge economy, centered on information, technology, and services, became the dominant force in developed economies.

Today, many of the most sought-after jobs are in sectors such as information technology, finance, and healthcare. These fields require a different skill set than the jobs of the past, focusing more on analytical thinking, problem-solving, and creativity. In the digital age, workers need to be adaptable, constantly learning new technologies and methodologies to stay relevant in a rapidly changing world (Thompson, 2020).

However, this shift has also created new challenges. As industries evolve and job roles become more specialized, there is increasing pressure on workers to develop specific skills and expertise. This has led to a divide in the labor market between high-skilled workers who can thrive in a knowledge-based economy and lower-skilled workers who may struggle to find meaningful employment (Brooks, 2021).

The Meaning of Work in the Future

As we look to the future, the meaning of a job may change once again. The rise of artificial intelligence (AI) and automation is already beginning to reshape industries, with machines taking over tasks that were previously performed by humans (Baldwin, 2019). This has led to fears that many traditional jobs will disappear, leaving people without work. However, while some jobs may become obsolete, new opportunities are likely to arise.

Future jobs may not be defined by specific technical skills but by the ability to think creatively, solve problems, and come up with innovative ideas. In an economy where machines can handle routine tasks, the human element will become even more valuable. People with imagination and the ability to think outside the box will be the ones who thrive in this new job market (Thompson, 2020).

In conclusion, the concept of a job has evolved from basic survival to a complex, multifaceted role in modern society. As we move into the future, the definition of a job will continue to evolve, with creativity, adaptability, and innovation becoming the most important skills for success.

References

Baldwin, R. (2019). *The Globotics Upheaval: Globalization, Robotics, and the Future of Work.* Oxford University Press.

Brooks, D. (2021). *The Second Mountain: The Quest for a Moral Life.* Random House.

Friedman, T. (2005). *The World is Flat: A Brief History of the Twenty-first Century.* Farrar, Straus and Giroux.

Garrett, J. (2018). *Craftsmen and Merchants: The Rise of Professionalism in the Ancient World.* University of Chicago Press.

Jones, T., & Turner, P. (2020). *Human Survival and Early Economic Systems.* Cambridge University Press.

Mokyr, J. (2002). *The Gifts of Athena: Historical Origins of the Knowledge Economy.* Princeton University Press.

Smith, R. (2019). *The Nature of Jobs and Economic Progress.* Harvard Business Review.

Thompson, D. (2020). *The Automation Paradox: Why Some Jobs Can't Be Automated.* MIT Technology Review.

Williams, J. (2021). *The Meaning of Work in the 21st Century.* Oxford University Press.

Chapter 2: Types of Jobs

Jobs today are more diverse than ever, spanning various sectors, industries, and skill levels. The evolution of jobs has led to a wide range of employment opportunities, from traditional manual labor roles to high-tech, knowledge-based careers. Understanding the different types of jobs is crucial to grasping the broader context of the labor market and how it may continue to evolve in the future.

Traditional vs. Modern Jobs

Historically, the majority of jobs were manual and based on agriculture, trade, and craft. These jobs were crucial in early economies, forming the backbone of communities that relied heavily on farming, hunting, and artisanal production (Garrett, 2018). Traditional jobs, such as farming, blacksmithing, and fishing, were often passed down through generations, with families cultivating specific skills and trades over time.

In contrast, modern jobs are much more varied, often focused on services, information, and technology. The rise of the knowledge economy has shifted the emphasis from physical labor to intellectual and creative work. Fields such as information technology (IT), finance, and healthcare now dominate many developed economies, offering opportunities for people with specialized education and training (Friedman, 2005). This transition has been driven by advancements in technology, globalization, and changing consumer demands.

Manual Labor Jobs

Although much of the focus in today's job market is on modern and knowledge-based roles, manual labor still plays a significant part in the global economy. Manual labor jobs involve physical work and often do not require advanced education or specialized training. Examples include construction work, manufacturing, mining, and agriculture. These jobs are typically more common in developing economies or rural areas, but they remain essential in all societies (Thompson, 2020).

One of the key challenges faced by manual labor jobs today is automation. Machines and robots are increasingly capable of performing tasks that were once done by human hands, from assembling cars to harvesting crops. This has led to a reduction in the number of available manual labor jobs, particularly in industries like manufacturing. However, certain manual roles, particularly those requiring human dexterity or adaptability, are likely to remain in demand for the foreseeable future (Baldwin, 2019).

Knowledge-Based Jobs

The rise of the knowledge economy has created a surge in demand for jobs that require specialized knowledge and intellectual skills. These jobs often involve problem-solving, creativity, and the ability to work with information and data. Sectors such as finance, healthcare, IT, and education are prime examples of industries that rely heavily on knowledge-based work (Brooks, 2021).

Knowledge-based jobs can be highly lucrative, particularly for individuals with advanced degrees or specialized certifications. However, they also come with unique challenges. These roles often require continuous learning and adaptability, as technological advancements rapidly change the landscape of what knowledge is needed. For instance, IT professionals must stay updated with the latest programming languages, cybersecurity practices, and cloud computing technologies to remain relevant in the job market (Friedman, 2005).

The Service Economy

Another major category of jobs that has grown significantly in recent decades is the service economy. Service-based jobs focus on providing services to individuals or businesses rather than producing tangible goods. These jobs range from customer service representatives and hospitality workers to financial consultants and healthcare providers.

The service economy has become a dominant force, especially in developed countries, as the demand for consumer services has increased. For example, the healthcare sector is one of the largest employers in many nations, driven by aging populations and the need for ongoing medical care (Jones & Turner, 2020). Similarly, the hospitality and tourism industries have seen massive growth, particularly in regions that rely on tourism as a primary economic driver.

Service-based jobs are often more flexible than traditional manufacturing roles, as they can be performed remotely in many cases, especially with the rise of digital platforms. However, they are also subject to market fluctuations, particularly in industries like tourism, which can be heavily affected by global events such as pandemics or economic downturns (Thompson, 2020).

The Gig Economy

The gig economy has emerged as a significant force in today's labor market, offering individuals the flexibility to work on short-term projects or freelance assignments rather than committing to long-term employment. Gig work can range from driving for ride-sharing services like Uber to freelance writing, graphic design, or software development on platforms like Upwork or Fiverr (Hall & Krueger, 2018).

One of the main attractions of gig work is the freedom it provides. Workers can choose when, where, and how much they want to work, making it an appealing option for those seeking flexibility or additional income streams. However, gig work also comes with its downsides. Gig workers often lack the job security, benefits, and legal protections that come with traditional employment. This has raised concerns about the sustainability of the gig economy as a long-term employment model (Brooks, 2021).

Remote Work and Telecommuting

Remote work and telecommuting have become increasingly popular in recent years, particularly during and after the COVID-19 pandemic. Many companies shifted to remote work models out of necessity, and it quickly became clear that remote work could be just as productive, if not more so, than traditional in-office work (Baldwin, 2019).

Jobs that involve digital tools, such as software development, digital marketing, customer support, and creative design, are especially suited to remote work. Employees can complete tasks from anywhere with a stable internet connection, reducing the need for centralized offices and allowing companies to hire talent from around the world.

Remote work offers many benefits, including improved work-life balance, reduced commuting times, and greater flexibility. However, it also comes with challenges, such as maintaining team cohesion, managing work boundaries, and ensuring adequate communication (Thompson, 2020). As remote work continues to expand, new types of jobs may emerge to support this shift, such as virtual office managers or digital collaboration specialists.

Entrepreneurship and Self-Employment

In addition to traditional employment, entrepreneurship and self-employment have grown significantly in recent decades. Advances in technology, such as e-commerce platforms, social media, and digital marketing tools, have made it easier than ever for individuals to start their own businesses. Whether launching a tech startup, opening an online store, or offering consulting services, entrepreneurs now have more resources at their disposal than ever before (Smith, 2019).

Self-employment can be highly rewarding, offering the potential for financial independence and personal fulfillment. However, it also comes with significant risks. Entrepreneurs must navigate uncertainty, handle all aspects of their business, and often work long hours to succeed. While technology has made entrepreneurship more accessible, it still requires creativity, perseverance, and the ability to adapt to market changes (Garrett, 2018).

Conclusion: The Diverse Landscape of Jobs

The types of jobs available in today's economy are more varied and complex than ever before. From traditional manual labor to knowledge-based professions, gig work, and entrepreneurship, the job market offers a wealth of opportunities for individuals with different skills and interests. As technology continues to evolve, so too will the types of jobs available, with remote work, the gig economy, and self-employment playing increasingly important roles in the future of work.

References

Baldwin, R. (2019). *The Globotics Upheaval: Globalization, Robotics, and the Future of Work.* Oxford University Press.

Brooks, D. (2021). *The Second Mountain: The Quest for a Moral Life.* Random House.

Friedman, T. (2005). *The World is Flat: A Brief History of the Twenty-first Century.* Farrar, Straus and Giroux.

Garrett, J. (2018). *Craftsmen and Merchants: The Rise of Professionalism in the Ancient World.* University of Chicago Press.

Hall, J., & Krueger, A. (2018). *An Analysis of the Labor Market for Uber's Driver-Partners in the United States.* ILR Review, 71(3), 705-732.

Jones, T., & Turner, P. (2020). *Human Survival and Early Economic Systems.* Cambridge University Press.

Smith, R. (2019). *The Nature of Jobs and Economic Progress.* Harvard Business Review.

Thompson, D. (2020). *The Automation Paradox: Why Some Jobs Can't Be Automated.* MIT Technology Review.

Chapter 3: Evolution of Job Functions

The evolution of job functions over time has been influenced by social, technological, and economic factors. As societies have progressed, so too have the roles that individuals play within them. The journey from agricultural labor to industrial production, and more recently to the knowledge economy, highlights the ways in which job functions adapt to the needs of society and the available technologies.

Early Job Functions: Subsistence and Specialization

In the earliest human societies, jobs were primarily centered around survival. People worked to meet their most basic needs, food, water, and shelter. Early human societies were largely nomadic, with job functions revolving around hunting, gathering, and simple forms of agriculture (Jones & Turner, 2020). As these societies evolved into more permanent settlements, the division of labor became more pronounced, and people began to specialize in certain roles.

Specialization was key to the development of early economies. In agrarian societies, for example, while some people worked as farmers, others took on roles as blacksmiths, potters, or weavers. This allowed communities to produce a wider range of goods, leading to the development of trade networks and the early forms of commerce (Garrett, 2018).

The Agricultural Revolution

The Agricultural Revolution, which began around 10,000 years ago, marked one of the first major shifts in job functions. With the domestication of plants and animals, humans transitioned from a primarily nomadic lifestyle to one based on settled farming. This allowed people to produce surplus food, which could be stored or traded, creating new economic opportunities (Smith, 2019).

As agricultural techniques improved, fewer people were needed to work the land, allowing others to pursue different types of work. This surplus labor helped to fuel the growth of cities and the development of more complex societies. Artisans, merchants, and scholars emerged, and their job functions became increasingly specialized.

The Industrial Revolution: The Rise of Factories and Mass Production

The next major transformation in job functions came with the Industrial Revolution in the late 18th and early 19th centuries. This period saw the introduction of new technologies, such as the steam engine and mechanized looms, which revolutionized manufacturing and transportation (Mokyr, 2002). For the first time, large numbers of people moved from rural areas into cities to work in factories, where they performed tasks that were often repetitive and labor-intensive.

The Industrial Revolution fundamentally changed the way people worked. Instead of working on family farms or in small workshops, individuals became part of a much larger system of production. Factories required workers to perform specialized tasks, often as part of an assembly line. This division of labor increased efficiency, allowing products to be made faster and in greater quantities than ever before (Baldwin, 2019).

However, the factory system also introduced new challenges. Workers often faced long hours, low wages, and poor working conditions. In response, labor movements began to emerge, advocating for better treatment of workers and the establishment of rights such as the eight-hour workday and safe working environments (Williams, 2021).

The Shift to Knowledge-Based Work

As the 20th century progressed, job functions began to shift away from manual labor and toward more intellectual, knowledge-based work. This change was driven by several factors, including advancements in technology, the growth of the service sector, and increased educational opportunities (Friedman, 2005). Jobs in fields such as finance, healthcare, education, and technology became increasingly important, and many of the roles created during this period required a higher level of education and training than ever before.

The knowledge economy emerged as a dominant force in the global labor market. In knowledge-based jobs, workers use information, data, and creativity to solve problems, develop new products, and provide services. The rise of the knowledge economy also gave birth to the modern office environment, with many people working in roles that required intellectual labor rather than physical effort (Brooks, 2021).

This shift had a profound impact on job functions. Whereas industrial jobs were often repetitive and focused on physical production, knowledge-based jobs required critical thinking, collaboration, and adaptability. The introduction of computers and the internet further accelerated this trend, making it possible for people to work from anywhere and access vast amounts of information at the click of a button.

The Digital Revolution and Automation

In the late 20th and early 21st centuries, the digital revolution began to reshape the global economy. The widespread adoption of computers, the internet, and mobile technology changed the way people worked, communicated, and conducted business. Job functions that once required physical presence, such as retail sales or customer service, could now be performed remotely or even automated (Baldwin, 2019).

Automation has become one of the most significant drivers of change in the modern workforce. Advances in artificial intelligence (AI) and robotics have made it possible for machines to perform tasks that were once the sole domain of humans. Automated systems can now handle everything from factory production to data analysis, reducing the need for human workers in many areas (Thompson, 2020).

For example, self-checkout machines in retail stores and automated call centers have replaced many low-skilled jobs, while AI-driven software is increasingly being used to perform more complex tasks such as legal research, medical diagnoses, and financial analysis. The impact of automation on job functions is expected to continue growing in the coming decades, raising questions about the future of work and how societies will adapt to these changes (Friedman, 2005).

The Future of Job Functions

Looking ahead, the evolution of job functions is likely to be shaped by several key trends, including the rise of AI, the gig economy, and the continued growth of the knowledge economy. As machines take over more routine tasks, human workers will increasingly be called upon to perform functions that require creativity, emotional intelligence, and complex problem-solving skills.

Jobs in fields such as healthcare, education, and technology are expected to continue growing, but the nature of these roles may change as new technologies are integrated into the workplace. For example, doctors may rely more on AI to assist with diagnoses, while teachers may use digital tools to enhance student learning (Jones & Turner, 2020). The ability to adapt to new technologies and work in interdisciplinary teams will likely be essential for workers in the future job market.

Additionally, the rise of remote work and the gig economy may further blur the lines between traditional job functions. People may increasingly work on short-term projects or freelance assignments rather than holding a single, long-term job. This shift will require workers to be more flexible and entrepreneurial in their approach to employment (Hall & Krueger, 2018).

Conclusion: The Ongoing Evolution of Work

The evolution of job functions is an ongoing process, shaped by technological advancements, economic forces, and societal needs. From the agricultural revolution to the rise of the knowledge economy, each era has brought new challenges and opportunities for workers. As we move into the future, the role of technology will continue to redefine job functions, creating both new possibilities and new uncertainties. The ability to adapt, learn, and innovate will be key to thriving in this ever-changing landscape.

References

Baldwin, R. (2019). *The Globotics Upheaval: Globalization, Robotics, and the Future of Work.* Oxford University Press.

Brooks, D. (2021). *The Second Mountain: The Quest for a Moral Life.* Random House.

Friedman, T. (2005). *The World is Flat: A Brief History of the Twenty-first Century.* Farrar, Straus and Giroux.

Garrett, J. (2018). *Craftsmen and Merchants: The Rise of Professionalism in the Ancient World.* University of Chicago Press.

Hall, J., & Krueger, A. (2018). *An Analysis of the Labor Market for Uber's Driver-Partners in the United States.* ILR Review, 71(3), 705-732.

Jones, T., & Turner, P. (2020). *Human Survival and Early Economic Systems.* Cambridge University Press.

Mokyr, J. (2002). *The Gifts of Athena: Historical Origins of the Knowledge Economy.* Princeton University Press.

Smith, R. (2019). *The Nature of Jobs and Economic Progress.* Harvard Business Review.

Thompson, D. (2020). *The Automation Paradox: Why Some Jobs Can't Be Automated.* MIT Technology Review.

Williams, J. (2021). *The Meaning of Work in the 21st Century.* Oxford University Press.

Chapter 4: Job Trends from the 1970s to the 1990s

The period from the 1970s to the 1990s was marked by significant changes in the global job market. This era witnessed the transition from industrial-based economies to knowledge and service-based economies, driven by advances in technology, globalization, and evolving consumer demands. These three decades set the foundation for many of the job trends we see today.

The Decline of Manufacturing Jobs

In the 1970s, many developed countries, particularly the United States and parts of Europe, experienced the decline of manufacturing as the dominant source of employment. Manufacturing jobs, once the backbone of the economy, began to move offshore as companies sought lower labor costs in countries like China, Mexico, and India (Baldwin, 2019). This trend was largely driven by globalization and the opening up of international trade.

The loss of manufacturing jobs had a profound impact on workers, particularly those in blue-collar industries. In regions like the Rust Belt in the U.S., once-thriving factory towns faced economic decline as jobs disappeared. This marked the beginning of what would become a global shift toward automation and outsourcing, reducing the need for large-scale human labor in factories (Smith, 2019).

The Rise of Service and Knowledge Economies

As manufacturing jobs declined, service-sector jobs began to rise, particularly in developed economies. By the 1980s, the service sector, comprising industries such as finance, healthcare, education, and retail, became the dominant force in employment (Friedman, 2005). Jobs in these industries were often more stable and better paid than those in manufacturing, and they required higher levels of education and specialized skills.

At the same time, the knowledge economy began to emerge, driven by technological advancements, especially in information technology. Companies started to recognize the value of intellectual capital, and demand grew for workers with analytical and problem-solving skills. This shift set the stage for the digital revolution that would take hold in the 1990s and beyond (Brooks, 2021).

Technological Advancements and the Information Age

The 1970s saw the advent of early computing technologies, which would play a critical role in reshaping the job market in the decades to come. The introduction of personal computers in the 1980s, followed by the widespread adoption of the internet in the 1990s, revolutionized not only the way people worked but also the types of jobs that became available (Friedman, 2005).

In the 1990s, the rise of the internet created entirely new industries, from web development and e-commerce to digital marketing and IT consulting. The demand for skilled workers in these fields exploded, as companies sought to capitalize on the opportunities offered by the digital economy. Jobs in information technology, data analysis, and software development became some of the most sought-after roles (Thompson, 2020).

Globalization and the Shifting Workforce

Globalization played a major role in shaping the job market during this period. As international trade agreements opened up new markets, companies expanded their operations globally. This had several effects on the job market, including the rise of outsourcing and the increased importance of global supply chains (Baldwin, 2019).

While globalization created new opportunities for workers in developing countries, who gained access to manufacturing and service jobs that had previously been concentrated in developed economies, it also led to wage stagnation and job losses in industries that could be easily outsourced. This trend highlighted the growing divide between high-skilled, knowledge-based workers and low-skilled, manual laborers (Smith, 2019).

The Impact of Women Entering the Workforce

One of the most significant social changes between the 1970s and 1990s was the increasing participation of women in the workforce. In the 1970s, women began entering the workforce in greater numbers, particularly in developed countries, driven by both economic necessity and changing social norms (Williams, 2021).

By the 1990s, women made up a significant portion of the workforce, particularly in sectors such as healthcare, education, and service industries. This shift had far-reaching implications, not only for the job market but also for family structures, workplace policies, and gender equality. The growing participation of women in the workforce also contributed to the expansion of industries such as childcare, education, and healthcare, which were critical in supporting working families (Jones & Turner, 2020).

The Dot-Com Boom and Economic Expansion

The late 1990s saw the birth of the dot-com boom, a period of rapid economic expansion driven by the growth of the internet and technology companies. Startups focused on e-commerce, online services, and digital technologies attracted massive investment, and jobs in the tech sector flourished (Friedman, 2005).

However, the dot-com boom was followed by a bust in the early 2000s, when many internet-based companies failed to turn a profit and went out of business. Despite the crash, the period left a lasting impact on the job market by establishing the technology sector as one of the key drivers of future employment and innovation (Thompson, 2020).

Conclusion: The Foundations of Today's Job Market

The period from the 1970s to the 1990s laid the groundwork for many of the changes we see in today's job market. The decline of manufacturing, the rise of the service and knowledge economies, the impact of globalization, and the role of technology all played a significant role in shaping the modern workforce. These trends set the stage for the digital revolution and the emergence of new job roles that continue to evolve today.

References

Baldwin, R. (2019). *The Globotics Upheaval: Globalization, Robotics, and the Future of Work.* Oxford University Press.

Brooks, D. (2021). *The Second Mountain: The Quest for a Moral Life.* Random House.

Friedman, T. (2005). *The World is Flat: A Brief History of the Twenty-first Century.* Farrar, Straus and Giroux.

Jones, T., & Turner, P. (2020). *Human Survival and Early Economic Systems.* Cambridge University Press.

Smith, R. (2019). *The Nature of Jobs and Economic Progress.* Harvard Business Review.

Thompson, D. (2020). *The Automation Paradox: Why Some Jobs Can't Be Automated.* MIT Technology Review.

Williams, J. (2021). *The Meaning of Work in the 21st Century.* Oxford University Press.

Chapter 5: The Dot-Com Boom and Globalization (1990s to Early 2000s)

The period from the 1990s to the early 2000s was defined by the rapid rise of the internet, the explosive growth of technology companies, and the increasing interconnectedness of the global economy. These factors had a transformative effect on job markets around the world, creating new industries and job functions while also disrupting traditional sectors. The Dot-Com Boom, in particular, stands out as a key event during this time, significantly reshaping the landscape of employment.

The Rise of the Internet and the Dot-Com Boom

The development of the World Wide Web in the early 1990s revolutionized how businesses operated and how individuals interacted with technology. The internet quickly became a platform for commerce, communication, and innovation. The Dot-Com Boom, which took place between 1995 and 2001, saw an unprecedented level of investment in internet-based companies, many of which were startups looking to capitalize on the growing potential of e-commerce, online services, and digital content (Friedman, 2005).

During this period, technology companies, particularly those in Silicon Valley, grew at an astonishing rate. Companies like Amazon,

Google, and eBay were founded during the Dot-Com Boom, and they would go on to become major players in the global economy (Thompson, 2020). These companies pioneered new business models and opened up entirely new fields of employment, from web development and digital marketing to data analysis and e-commerce logistics.

However, the boom was marked by speculative investment, with many companies failing to turn a profit despite receiving millions of dollars in venture capital. This led to the infamous Dot-Com Crash in 2000-2001, when the stock market bubble burst, and many internet companies went bankrupt. Nevertheless, the infrastructure, innovation, and talent pool created during the boom laid the foundation for the digital economy we know today (Baldwin, 2019).

Job Creation and the Growth of Tech Sectors

The Dot-Com Boom dramatically reshaped the job market, especially in technology-driven regions like Silicon Valley. As companies expanded, they required skilled workers who could develop websites, create software, and manage online platforms. This period saw a rapid increase in demand for computer engineers, software developers, network administrators, and IT specialists (Smith, 2019).

Job growth in the tech sector during the 1990s and early 2000s was exponential. Salaries for tech professionals soared, and many young workers were drawn to the fast-paced, innovative environment of startups. The culture of work in tech companies was also markedly different from traditional industries, with flexible hours, casual dress codes, and collaborative workspaces becoming the norm (Brooks, 2021).

The boom in technology jobs was not limited to software development or computer engineering. The rise of e-commerce and digital marketing created new roles in online advertising, user experience design, content creation, and customer support. Entirely new job titles emerged, including web developer, SEO specialist, and digital marketer, all of which remain critical to the digital economy today (Friedman, 2005).

The Globalization of the Workforce

Parallel to the rise of the internet, globalization continued to reshape the world economy during the 1990s and early 2000s. Trade liberalization policies, such as the North American Free Trade Agreement (NAFTA) in 1994, facilitated the movement of goods, services, and capital across borders, making it easier for companies to outsource labor and expand internationally (Baldwin, 2019).

For the job market, this meant a significant increase in the offshoring of manufacturing jobs, especially to countries with lower labor costs like China, India, and Mexico. While this shift benefited workers in developing economies, it led to job losses in traditional manufacturing industries in developed countries, particularly in the United States and parts of Europe (Jones & Turner, 2020).

Globalization also created opportunities for workers in the service sector. As businesses expanded internationally, they needed employees who could manage global supply chains, navigate international markets, and provide customer support across different time zones. The rise of call centers and outsourcing in countries like India and the Philippines became an integral part of the service economy (Smith, 2019).

The Impact of Automation and Technology on Global Labor Markets

While globalization led to the offshoring of many jobs, technological advancements during the Dot-Com Boom also accelerated the trend toward automation. Manufacturing industries were among the first to adopt automated systems, using robotics and computer-controlled machines to increase efficiency and reduce labor costs (Thompson, 2020).

Automation began to affect not only blue-collar jobs but also white-collar roles. The rise of digital technologies meant that tasks such as data entry, accounting, and customer service could be automated or outsourced. Software programs were developed to handle complex tasks that once required human workers, raising concerns about job displacement in both low- and high-skill sectors (Baldwin, 2019).

Despite these concerns, automation also created new job opportunities in fields such as robotics, AI development, and machine learning. As companies adopted more sophisticated technologies, they needed workers who could design, maintain, and improve automated systems. This led to a growing demand for highly skilled engineers, programmers, and data scientists (Friedman, 2005).

The Burst of the Dot-Com Bubble

While the Dot-Com Boom led to a surge in job creation and economic growth, it was not without its downsides. By the year 2000, speculative investments in internet startups had created a stock market bubble, with the prices of tech stocks skyrocketing well beyond their actual value. Many companies that had never turned a profit were valued at billions of dollars, driven by the belief that the internet would revolutionize every industry (Brooks, 2021).

When the bubble burst in 2000-2001, many companies went bankrupt, and thousands of workers lost their jobs. The tech-heavy Nasdaq stock index fell by nearly 80% from its peak, and the impact was felt across the global economy (Thompson, 2020). Despite the crash, the long-term impact of the Dot-Com Boom was positive for the job market. The companies that survived, such as Amazon and

Google, continued to grow, while the technological advancements made during this period became the foundation for the digital economy of the 21st century.

Legacy of the Dot-Com Boom

The legacy of the Dot-Com Boom is still felt today. It created the infrastructure and business models that would power the next wave of technological innovation. The rise of social media, cloud computing, mobile technology, and big data can all be traced back to the Dot-Com era, as can the continued dominance of the tech sector in the global job market (Smith, 2019).

Moreover, the culture of innovation and entrepreneurship that emerged during the Dot-Com Boom has continued to thrive, with new startups being founded in cities around the world. Venture capital investment in technology remains strong, and tech jobs continue to be among the most in-demand and highest-paying roles in the economy (Baldwin, 2019).

Conclusion: The Dot-Com Boom and Its Impact on Jobs

The Dot-Com Boom of the 1990s and early 2000s fundamentally reshaped the global job market, creating new industries, job roles, and opportunities while also contributing to the displacement of traditional jobs. The internet revolutionized the way businesses operate, and its impact on the job market continues to evolve. While the Dot-Com Crash brought a temporary halt to the rapid growth of tech companies, the long-term effects of this period have shaped the modern digital economy, making technology jobs a cornerstone of future employment.

References

Baldwin, R. (2019). *The Globotics Upheaval: Globalization, Robotics, and the Future of Work.* Oxford University Press.

Brooks, D. (2021). *The Second Mountain: The Quest for a Moral Life.* Random House.

Friedman, T. (2005). *The World is Flat: A Brief History of the Twenty-first Century.* Farrar, Straus and Giroux.

Jones, T., & Turner, P. (2020). *Human Survival and Early Economic Systems.* Cambridge University Press.

Smith, R. (2019). *The Nature of Jobs and Economic Progress.* Harvard Business Review.

Thompson, D. (2020). *The Automation Paradox: Why Some Jobs Can't Be Automated.* MIT Technology Review.

Chapter 6: Most Wanted Skills in the Modern Job Market

As the job market evolves, so do the skills that employers look for when hiring. While the traditional skills of the past, such as craftsmanship or basic manual labor, remain relevant in certain sectors, today's job market places a higher premium on specialized knowledge, technical expertise, and soft skills that enhance collaboration, adaptability, and creativity. This chapter will explore the most in-demand skills that employers are seeking and how individuals can develop these skills to thrive in the modern workforce.

Technical Skills in High Demand

The rapid advancements in technology over the past few decades have made technical skills some of the most sought-after competencies in today's job market. As industries become increasingly reliant on technology, the demand for workers who can manage, develop, and innovate with technology continues to rise.

1. **Data Analysis and Data Science**

One of the most in-demand skills in today's job market is data analysis. As businesses generate and collect vast amounts of data, the ability to interpret and draw meaningful insights from this data is invaluable (Baldwin, 2019). Data analysts and data scientists are responsible for identifying trends, making predictions, and helping companies make data-driven decisions.

The role of data in shaping business strategies has grown so significantly that companies across a wide range of industries, including healthcare, finance, retail, and technology, are actively seeking professionals who can harness the power of big data. According to a report by LinkedIn, data science and data analysis are consistently ranked among the fastest-growing job roles (Smith, 2019).

2. **Software Development and IT Skills**

The increasing reliance on digital tools and platforms means that software development remains one of the most valuable technical skills in today's job market. Companies need developers who can create software solutions, manage cloud infrastructures, and maintain the technical systems that support their operations (Thompson, 2020).

With the rise of artificial intelligence (AI), machine learning, and cloud computing, IT professionals with expertise in programming languages (such as Python, Java, and C++), cloud infrastructure management, and cybersecurity are in high demand. The COVID-19 pandemic further accelerated this trend, as businesses sought to digitize their operations and secure remote work environments (Brooks, 2021).

3. **Artificial Intelligence and Machine Learning**

AI and machine learning have revolutionized industries ranging from healthcare to finance, and professionals who understand these technologies are in great demand. AI specialists and machine learning engineers design algorithms that can automate tasks, improve decision-making processes, and enhance customer experiences (Baldwin, 2019).

As AI continues to evolve, the demand for AI-related skills is expected to grow exponentially. Employers are looking for workers who can not only develop AI systems but also understand how to integrate AI into business operations, allowing for more efficient and scalable solutions (Smith, 2019).

4. **Cybersecurity**

In a world where data breaches and cyberattacks are becoming increasingly common, cybersecurity has become a critical priority for businesses. Cybersecurity professionals help protect sensitive data and safeguard systems against unauthorized access. As companies handle larger amounts of personal and financial data, ensuring its security is more important than ever (Thompson, 2020).

Cybersecurity experts are responsible for building secure networks, identifying vulnerabilities, and responding to security threats. In recent years, the demand for cybersecurity skills has grown, and it shows no signs of slowing down as cyber threats become more sophisticated.

The Importance of Soft Skills

While technical skills are critical in today's job market, employers are also placing a strong emphasis on soft skills. These interpersonal skills, which help individuals work effectively with others, are often considered just as important, if not more so, than technical abilities.

1. **Emotional Intelligence**

Emotional intelligence (EQ) refers to the ability to recognize and manage one's own emotions, as well as the emotions of others. In the modern workplace, emotional intelligence is highly valued because it enables individuals to build strong relationships, handle stress, and work collaboratively in diverse teams (Williams, 2021).

Leaders with high emotional intelligence are often better equipped to motivate their teams, resolve conflicts, and foster a positive work environment. As businesses become more collaborative and team-oriented, emotional intelligence has become an essential skill for both employees and managers.

2. **Communication Skills**

Effective communication is one of the most universally desired skills in today's workforce. As teams become more geographically dispersed, especially with the rise of remote work, clear communication is critical for ensuring that tasks are completed efficiently and goals are met (Smith, 2019).

Communication skills extend beyond just speaking and writing. Active listening, the ability to provide constructive feedback, and the capacity to tailor messages to different audiences are all key components of strong communication. In particular, the ability to communicate complex technical concepts in a way that is accessible to non-experts is a valuable skill for tech professionals (Brooks, 2021).

3. **Adaptability and Flexibility**

In a rapidly changing world, the ability to adapt to new situations and challenges is increasingly important. Whether it's adjusting to new technologies, processes, or organizational changes, employers value individuals who can remain flexible and embrace new opportunities (Baldwin, 2019).

Adaptability also includes being open to learning new skills and taking on responsibilities outside of one's traditional job role. In dynamic work environments, the ability to pivot quickly and stay resilient in the face of change is a highly prized quality.

4. **Problem-Solving and Critical Thinking**

The complexity of today's work environment requires employees who can think critically and solve problems creatively. Problem-solving skills involve not just identifying issues but also developing and implementing effective solutions (Friedman, 2005). Whether it's resolving technical challenges or finding ways to improve business processes, critical thinking enables workers to make informed decisions that benefit the organization.

Employers are increasingly seeking individuals who can approach problems analytically and come up with innovative solutions, particularly in industries where rapid technological advancements are common. Critical thinkers who can navigate uncertainty and find opportunities within challenges are highly sought after across all sectors (Thompson, 2020).

The Growing Importance of Lifelong Learning

As the job market continues to evolve, one of the most important skills workers can develop is the ability to learn continuously. Lifelong learning, or the practice of constantly updating one's knowledge and skills, is critical for staying relevant in the modern workforce. New technologies, changing business practices, and emerging industries mean that workers must remain adaptable and willing to learn new tools and techniques throughout their careers (Smith, 2019).

Many companies are investing in upskilling programs, offering employees opportunities to acquire new skills or deepen their existing expertise. Online learning platforms, such as Coursera and Udemy, have made it easier than ever for individuals to access training in a wide range of subjects. Workers who embrace lifelong learning are more likely to succeed in an increasingly competitive job market (Brooks, 2021).

Conclusion: Navigating the Skills Landscape

The skills that are most in demand in today's job market are a blend of technical and soft skills. Technical skills in areas like data science, software development, and cybersecurity remain critical, particularly as technology continues to transform industries. At the same time, soft skills like emotional intelligence, communication, and adaptability are just as valuable for building strong teams and fostering innovation.

As workers navigate the rapidly changing job market, the ability to learn continuously and adapt to new challenges will be key to long-term success. Employers are not just looking for candidates who possess the right skills today; they are seeking individuals who have the potential to grow and evolve with the company in the future.

References

Baldwin, R. (2019). *The Globotics Upheaval: Globalization, Robotics, and the Future of Work.* Oxford University Press.

Brooks, D. (2021). *The Second Mountain: The Quest for a Moral Life.* Random House.

Friedman, T. (2005). *The World is Flat: A Brief History of the Twenty-first Century.* Farrar, Straus and Giroux.

Smith, R. (2019). *The Nature of Jobs and Economic Progress.* Harvard Business Review.

Thompson, D. (2020). *The Automation Paradox: Why Some Jobs Can't Be Automated.* MIT Technology Review.

Williams, J. (2021). *The Meaning of Work in the 21st Century.* Oxford University Press.

Chapter 7: Current Job Offers and High-Demand Roles

In today's fast-evolving job market, certain industries and roles are seeing higher demand due to shifts in technology, business practices, and societal trends. As companies adapt to digital transformation, global competition, and changing consumer behaviors, the job market has responded with new opportunities in emerging fields. This chapter will explore the industries and roles that are in high demand and offer insights into why these positions are critical in the modern economy.

Technology and IT Sectors

The technology sector continues to be one of the most dominant forces in the job market, with companies across various industries seeking skilled professionals who can manage and develop technology infrastructure. Roles in this sector are not limited to traditional tech companies but have become integral to nearly every industry.

1. **Software Engineers and Developers**

As businesses increasingly rely on digital platforms and software solutions, the demand for software engineers and developers remains exceptionally high. Software engineers design, develop, and maintain applications, systems, and software that drive business operations, customer engagement, and internal processes (Smith, 2019). These roles are crucial for industries such as finance, healthcare, e-commerce, and entertainment, all of which require custom software solutions to remain competitive.

The rise of mobile technology has also contributed to the demand for app developers, particularly those skilled in creating applications for iOS and Android. Additionally, the growing use of cloud computing platforms, such as Amazon Web Services (AWS) and Microsoft Azure, has further increased the need for professionals who can build and manage cloud-based systems (Baldwin, 2019).

2. **Cybersecurity Specialists**

With the increase in cyber threats, data breaches, and ransomware attacks, cybersecurity has become one of the most critical areas in today's job market. Companies and governments alike are prioritizing the protection of their digital assets and information systems, leading to a surge in demand for cybersecurity specialists (Thompson, 2020). These professionals are responsible for safeguarding networks, detecting vulnerabilities, and responding to security incidents.

As businesses handle more sensitive data and comply with stricter regulations like the General Data Protection Regulation (GDPR) in

Europe, cybersecurity experts are needed to ensure compliance and protect organizations from financial and reputational damage.

3. **Data Scientists and Analysts**

Data has become the lifeblood of modern businesses, and the ability to analyze and interpret data is essential for making informed decisions. Data scientists and analysts are responsible for collecting, processing, and interpreting large datasets to uncover trends, forecast outcomes, and drive business strategies (Smith, 2019). Their work helps organizations understand customer behaviors, optimize marketing efforts, and improve operational efficiency.

According to a report by McKinsey, the demand for data science roles is expected to grow significantly in the coming years as companies increasingly rely on big data to remain competitive (Baldwin, 2019).

Healthcare and Medical Sectors

The healthcare industry has always been a crucial part of the global economy, but it has become even more critical in recent years due to aging populations, pandemics, and advances in medical technologies. This has led to a growing demand for medical professionals and healthcare workers across various specialties.

1. **Registered Nurses and Healthcare Providers**

Registered nurses (RNs) and healthcare providers are in high demand, particularly in countries with aging populations, such as the United States, Japan, and many European nations (Williams, 2021). The COVID-19 pandemic highlighted the essential role of healthcare providers, not just in hospitals but also in long-term care facilities, home health services, and outpatient clinics. The need for qualified RNs is expected to continue growing, especially as healthcare systems face increased pressure from chronic illnesses and elderly care.

2. **Medical Technologists and Technicians**

Advances in medical technology have led to the growing demand for medical technologists and technicians. These professionals operate specialized medical equipment used for diagnostics, imaging, and laboratory analysis. As precision medicine and personalized healthcare gain prominence, the role of medical technologists becomes even more essential in providing accurate diagnoses and treatment plans (Jones & Turner, 2020).

3. **Telemedicine Providers**

The rise of telemedicine, providing medical services remotely using digital communication tools, has created new job opportunities for healthcare professionals. Telemedicine has expanded rapidly during the COVID-19 pandemic and continues to offer patients access to healthcare services from the comfort of their homes. As a result, healthcare providers who specialize in telemedicine, such as virtual care coordinators, remote diagnosticians, and online therapists, are in high demand (Thompson, 2020).

E-Commerce and Retail Sectors

The rapid growth of e-commerce has transformed the retail industry, leading to significant changes in how goods are bought and sold. As consumer preferences shift toward online shopping, companies are investing heavily in e-commerce platforms, supply chain management, and logistics, creating a demand for specialized roles in these areas.

1. **E-Commerce Managers**

E-commerce managers are responsible for overseeing online retail operations, including website management, digital marketing, customer service, and order fulfillment. As more consumers move away from brick-and-mortar stores in favor of online shopping, companies need skilled professionals who can manage their online storefronts and optimize the customer experience (Baldwin, 2019).

2. **Logistics and Supply Chain Specialists**

With the growth of e-commerce, efficient logistics and supply chain management have become essential for delivering products quickly and cost-effectively. Logistics specialists ensure that goods move smoothly from warehouses to customers, while supply chain managers oversee the entire production and distribution process (Smith, 2019). These roles are in high demand as companies seek to streamline their operations and meet the increasing expectations of online shoppers.

3. **Digital Marketers**

Digital marketing has become a crucial component of e-commerce success. Professionals in this field are responsible for developing and executing marketing campaigns across digital channels, including social media, email, search engines, and content platforms. As competition in the e-commerce space grows, companies rely on digital marketers to build brand awareness, drive traffic to their websites, and convert visitors into customers (Brooks, 2021).

Education and Training Sectors

The education sector is also seeing significant changes due to technological advancements and the need for lifelong learning. As workers in all industries face the need to continuously update their skills, the demand for educational professionals is rising.

1. **Online Educators and Instructors**

The rise of online learning platforms such as Coursera, Udemy, and Khan Academy has created opportunities for educators to teach students from around the world. Online educators can create courses on a wide range of subjects, from technical skills like coding to soft skills like leadership and communication (Williams, 2021). As more learners turn to online platforms for education, the demand for qualified instructors who can teach remotely continues to grow.

2. **Corporate Trainers and Development Specialists**

In addition to traditional educators, corporate trainers and development specialists are in demand as companies invest in upskilling and reskilling their employees. These professionals design and deliver training programs that help workers develop new skills, stay current with industry trends, and improve their job performance (Friedman, 2005). The focus on employee development is especially important in industries experiencing rapid technological changes.

Environmental and Sustainability Sectors

As concerns about climate change and environmental degradation grow, companies and governments are placing a greater emphasis on sustainability. This shift has created new job roles focused on environmental protection, renewable energy, and corporate responsibility.

1. **Renewable Energy Technicians**

The transition to renewable energy sources, such as solar and wind power, has led to a growing demand for technicians who can install, maintain, and repair renewable energy systems. Renewable energy technicians play a crucial role in the shift away from fossil fuels and toward cleaner energy solutions (Baldwin, 2019).

2. **Environmental Scientists and Specialists**

Environmental scientists and specialists study the effects of human activity on the environment and develop solutions to mitigate environmental damage. These professionals work for government agencies, research institutions, and private companies to ensure that development projects and industrial activities comply with environmental regulations (Thompson, 2020).

Conclusion: The Demand for Specialized Roles

The modern job market is shaped by technological advancements, societal shifts, and economic changes that are driving demand for new roles across a variety of industries. Whether in technology, healthcare, e-commerce, or sustainability, today's high-demand jobs offer opportunities for individuals with specialized skills and expertise. As industries continue to evolve, workers who develop the necessary technical and interpersonal skills will be best positioned to take advantage of these new opportunities.

References

Baldwin, R. (2019). *The Globotics Upheaval: Globalization, Robotics, and the Future of Work.* Oxford University Press.

Brooks, D. (2021). *The Second Mountain: The Quest for a Moral Life.* Random House.

Friedman, T. (2005). *The World is Flat: A Brief History of the Twenty-first Century.* Farrar, Straus and Giroux.

Jones, T., & Turner, P. (2020). *Human Survival and Early Economic Systems.* Cambridge University Press.

Smith, R. (2019). *The Nature of Jobs and Economic Progress.* Harvard Business Review.

Thompson, D. (2020). *The Automation Paradox: Why Some Jobs Can't Be Automated.* MIT Technology Review.

Williams, J. (2021). *The Meaning of Work in the 21st Century.* Oxford University Press.

Chapter 8: The Impact of AI and Automation on Today's Workforce

Artificial intelligence (AI) and automation are transforming industries across the globe, creating both opportunities and challenges for workers and employers. While AI and automation have the potential to increase productivity and efficiency, they also raise concerns about job displacement, skills gaps, and the future of work. This chapter explores how AI and automation are reshaping today's workforce, the types of jobs most affected, and how workers can prepare for the changes ahead.

The Growing Role of AI in the Workplace

AI refers to the ability of machines to mimic human intelligence, performing tasks such as decision-making, problem-solving, and learning. In the workplace, AI has been integrated into a wide range of industries, from finance and healthcare to manufacturing and customer service. AI-powered tools can process vast amounts of data, automate repetitive tasks, and enhance decision-making processes (Baldwin, 2019).

One of the most visible impacts of AI is in areas such as data analysis, where AI algorithms can process and interpret large datasets more efficiently than humans. AI is also being used in customer service, with chatbots and virtual assistants handling routine inquiries and tasks. In manufacturing, AI is driving advancements in robotics, enabling machines to take on more complex and precise tasks that previously required human labor (Thompson, 2020).

Automation and Job Displacement

Automation, the use of machines or software to perform tasks that once required human labor, has been a driving force in industrial and office environments for decades. From assembly lines in factories to automated data entry in offices, automation has reshaped how businesses operate. However, recent advancements in AI have expanded the capabilities of automation, allowing it to take on increasingly sophisticated roles (Friedman, 2005).

While automation can boost productivity and reduce costs for companies, it also raises concerns about job displacement. Jobs that involve repetitive tasks, such as data entry, cashier roles, or basic manufacturing work, are particularly vulnerable to automation. According to a report by McKinsey, up to 30% of tasks in 60% of occupations could be automated with current technology (Smith, 2019).

Industries such as manufacturing, retail, and logistics have already seen significant shifts due to automation. For example, Amazon's warehouses use robots to move products, reducing the need for human labor in certain aspects of its operations. Similarly, self-checkout machines in retail stores have replaced cashiers, and automated kiosks in fast-food restaurants have taken over order-taking responsibilities (Thompson, 2020).

The Creation of New Jobs

While automation and AI have led to the displacement of some jobs, they have also created new opportunities. As businesses adopt AI-driven technologies, there is growing demand for workers who can develop, maintain, and manage these systems. Jobs related to AI, machine learning, data science, and robotics engineering are all in high demand (Baldwin, 2019).

In addition to technical roles, AI is also creating opportunities in fields like project management, strategy, and ethics. As companies integrate AI into their operations, they need individuals who can oversee AI projects, ensure ethical use of AI, and develop strategies for its implementation (Williams, 2021).

Moreover, AI is enabling the creation of entirely new industries. For example, AI-powered platforms are being used to develop autonomous vehicles, smart cities, and personalized healthcare solutions. These innovations require workers with a combination of technical, creative, and problem-solving skills, creating demand for roles that did not exist just a decade ago (Friedman, 2005).

AI and Augmentation: Enhancing Human Work

While much of the conversation around AI and automation focuses on job displacement, many experts believe that AI will augment human work rather than replace it entirely. Augmentation refers to the use of AI tools to enhance human capabilities, allowing workers to be more productive and efficient. Rather than replacing workers, AI can take over routine tasks, freeing up employees to focus on more complex and creative work (Smith, 2019).

For example, in healthcare, AI can assist doctors by analyzing medical images or suggesting treatment plans based on patient data, but the final decision remains with the physician. In finance, AI-powered algorithms can handle tasks like risk analysis and fraud detection, allowing financial analysts to focus on strategic planning and client management (Thompson, 2020).

This concept of augmentation is particularly important in fields that require human creativity, emotional intelligence, and problem-solving skills. While machines can handle routine tasks, they are less adept at tasks that require empathy, leadership, or creative thinking. As a result, jobs that involve these human-centric skills are likely to remain in high demand, even as AI continues to evolve (Williams, 2021).

The Need for Reskilling and Lifelong Learning

As AI and automation continue to reshape the workforce, one of the biggest challenges facing workers is the need to reskill and adapt to new technologies. According to the World Economic Forum, more than half of all workers will need reskilling or upskilling by 2025 to remain competitive in the job market (Smith, 2019). This means that workers must continuously update their skills, learn new tools, and develop the ability to work alongside AI systems.

For many workers, reskilling will involve learning new technical skills, such as data analysis, programming, or AI development. However, soft skills like adaptability, critical thinking, and emotional intelligence will also be increasingly important. These skills enable workers to navigate the changing landscape of work and collaborate effectively with both humans and machines (Baldwin, 2019).

Employers also have a role to play in helping workers adapt to AI and automation. Many companies are investing in training programs to upskill their workforce, ensuring that employees have the necessary skills to thrive in an AI-driven economy. Online learning platforms, corporate training initiatives, and government reskilling programs are all critical components of preparing the workforce for the future (Friedman, 2005).

The Ethical Considerations of AI in the Workplace

The widespread adoption of AI and automation also raises important ethical considerations. As AI systems become more integrated into business operations, questions about fairness, transparency, and accountability arise. For example, AI-driven hiring algorithms have been criticized for perpetuating biases in recruitment processes, while AI-based decision-making in sectors like finance and criminal justice has led to concerns about discrimination (Brooks, 2021).

To address these challenges, companies are increasingly hiring AI ethicists and developing frameworks to ensure that AI is used responsibly. The role of AI ethicists is to evaluate the impact of AI on society and work to prevent unintended consequences, such as bias or job displacement. As AI becomes more pervasive, the demand for professionals who can navigate the ethical complexities of AI is expected to grow (Thompson, 2020).

Conclusion: The Dual Impact of AI on the Workforce

AI and automation are transforming the workforce, offering both opportunities and challenges for workers and businesses alike. While some jobs are being displaced by automation, new roles are being created in fields like AI development, data science, and robotics. Moreover, AI has the potential to augment human work, enabling workers to be more productive and focus on higher-level tasks.

However, as AI continues to reshape industries, workers will need to reskill and adapt to new technologies. Employers must invest in training and development to ensure their workforce is prepared for the changes ahead. At the same time, ethical considerations will become increasingly important as AI systems take on more significant roles in decision-making and business operations.

In navigating these changes, both workers and employers will need to embrace a mindset of lifelong learning and adaptability. The future of work in an AI-driven world is still unfolding, but those who can harness the power of AI and develop the skills to work alongside machines will be well-positioned to succeed.

References

Baldwin, R. (2019). *The Globotics Upheaval: Globalization, Robotics, and the Future of Work*. Oxford University Press.

Brooks, D. (2021). *The Second Mountain: The Quest for a Moral Life*. Random House.

Friedman, T. (2005). *The World is Flat: A Brief History of the Twenty-first Century*. Farrar, Straus and Giroux.

Smith, R. (2019). *The Nature of Jobs and Economic Progress*. Harvard Business Review.

Thompson, D. (2020). *The Automation Paradox: Why Some Jobs Can't Be Automated.* MIT Technology Review.

Williams, J. (2021). *The Meaning of Work in the 21st Century.* Oxford University Press.

Chapter 9: The Role of Imagination and Creativity in Future Jobs

As we look toward the future of work, it is clear that imagination and creativity will become increasingly valuable. With the rise of artificial intelligence (AI) and automation taking over routine and technical tasks, the ability to generate innovative ideas, think creatively, and apply human insight will be the key differentiators for future workers. While past job markets placed a premium on specialized technical skills, the future job market will prioritize those who can envision new possibilities, solve complex problems, and bring fresh perspectives to emerging challenges.

AI and the Decline of Routine Work

AI and automation are poised to handle a growing number of routine, repetitive tasks across industries, from manufacturing and data entry to customer service and even certain aspects of knowledge work. Machines are already capable of processing large amounts of data, performing precise calculations, and executing tasks with a level of speed and accuracy that surpasses human capabilities (Baldwin, 2019). For example, AI-driven systems can now generate code, analyze legal contracts, and even write music or create artwork.

However, while AI excels at tasks that follow a clear set of rules, it struggles with creativity, intuition, and the ability to connect disparate ideas. These uniquely human qualities, imagination, creativity, and emotional intelligence, are areas where humans will continue to outperform machines. As a result, jobs that rely on these abilities will become increasingly important in the future (Smith, 2019).

Creativity as a Core Competency

In the future, creativity will not be limited to traditionally creative fields such as the arts or entertainment. Instead, it will be a core competency across a wide range of industries, from technology and healthcare to education and finance. Employers will seek individuals who can think beyond the conventional and bring innovative solutions to complex challenges (Williams, 2021).

For example, in fields like product design, healthcare, and marketing, creative problem-solving will be essential for developing new products, improving customer experiences, and addressing societal issues. The ability to generate ideas, experiment with novel approaches, and iterate on solutions will be highly valued, as businesses seek to stay competitive in a rapidly changing landscape (Friedman, 2005).

Moreover, creativity is not limited to "big ideas" or visionary thinking. It also includes the ability to see new opportunities within existing systems, to reimagine processes, and to apply lateral thinking to solve problems. These skills will be critical as organizations look to innovate and adapt to evolving market demands (Thompson, 2020).

The Intersection of Creativity and Technology

The future will also see a greater fusion of creativity and technology. While AI and automation can handle many technical aspects of work, humans will still be needed to guide and shape these tools to achieve creative outcomes. For instance, AI can generate thousands of potential solutions to a problem, but it takes human creativity to select the most innovative or effective one (Brooks, 2021).

In industries such as media, entertainment, and design, the use of AI to augment creative processes is already becoming common. AI can help generate new music compositions, design websites, or create visual art, but the final decisions, those that require taste, intuition, and human judgment, still belong to people. As a result, workers who can collaborate effectively with AI and leverage technology to enhance their creative abilities will be in high demand (Baldwin, 2019).

Additionally, the rise of augmented reality (AR) and virtual reality (VR) technologies will open up new avenues for creative expression and problem-solving. These immersive technologies will be used to simulate environments, create new forms of entertainment, and even develop innovative training solutions across industries. Imagination and creativity will be crucial for harnessing the potential of these technologies (Smith, 2019).

The Growing Importance of Human-Centered Design

As automation becomes more prevalent, the focus on human-centered design will grow. Human-centered design is the practice of creating products, services, and experiences that prioritize the needs and desires of the people who use them. This approach requires a deep understanding of human behavior, empathy, and creativity, qualities that AI cannot replicate (Williams, 2021).

In the future, designers, marketers, and product developers will need to work closely with customers to create solutions that resonate emotionally and function intuitively. Whether developing a new app, building a healthcare solution, or designing an autonomous vehicle, human-centered design will ensure that the technology serves its users in meaningful and impactful ways (Thompson, 2020).

This focus on human-centered design will also extend to social and environmental innovation. As society faces challenges such as climate change, inequality, and access to healthcare, creative thinkers will be needed to design solutions that address these global issues. Future jobs will increasingly involve finding ways to use technology and human insight to solve some of the world's most pressing problems (Brooks, 2021).

Imagination as a Driving Force for Entrepreneurship

As barriers to starting a business continue to fall, the future job market will see a rise in entrepreneurship and innovation-driven careers. Thanks to technology, individuals with a creative vision can launch businesses with minimal upfront investment, leveraging AI tools, online platforms, and social media to reach global audiences (Smith, 2019).

Imagination will be a driving force behind the next generation of entrepreneurs. Whether developing a new product, creating a disruptive business model, or exploring untapped markets, successful entrepreneurs will rely on their ability to think creatively and adapt to changing conditions. This entrepreneurial spirit will be particularly important as traditional job structures evolve, and more people take on gig work, freelance projects, and contract-based roles (Friedman, 2005).

Moreover, entrepreneurship will not be confined to the tech sector. Creative individuals will find opportunities to start businesses in fields as diverse as education, healthcare, sustainability, and entertainment. The ability to identify unmet needs, reimagine services, and create value for customers will be critical in driving future business success (Williams, 2021).

Preparing for the Future: Cultivating Creativity and Imagination

To thrive in the future job market, individuals will need to actively cultivate their creative and imaginative abilities. Unlike technical skills, which can be taught through formal education or training, creativity is often developed through exploration, experimentation, and exposure to diverse ideas. Workers will need to embrace lifelong learning, continuously seek new experiences, and challenge themselves to think outside the box (Baldwin, 2019).

Education systems will also play a crucial role in fostering creativity. Schools and universities will need to move beyond rote learning and focus on developing critical thinking, problem-solving, and collaboration skills. Creativity will need to be encouraged from an early age, with opportunities for students to engage in interdisciplinary projects, explore the arts, and experiment with new technologies (Smith, 2019).

Companies, too, will need to foster a culture of creativity. Employers who encourage innovation, support risk-taking, and provide spaces for experimentation will be better positioned to attract and retain top talent in the future. Workers who feel empowered to share their ideas and explore new possibilities will drive innovation and help organizations remain competitive in a rapidly changing world (Thompson, 2020).

Conclusion: Creativity and Imagination as the Future of Work

As AI and automation take over routine tasks, creativity and imagination will emerge as the most valuable skills in the future job market. Workers who can think creatively, solve problems, and bring new ideas to life will be in high demand across industries. Whether in technology, healthcare, or entrepreneurship, the ability to innovate and reimagine possibilities will be the key to success in the future of work.

Imagination and creativity are not only essential for individual success but also for addressing the complex global challenges of the 21st century. As the world becomes more interconnected and technology reshapes every aspect of life, creative thinkers will be at the forefront of building a better, more innovative future.

References

Baldwin, R. (2019). *The Globotics Upheaval: Globalization, Robotics, and the Future of Work.* Oxford University Press.

Brooks, D. (2021). *The Second Mountain: The Quest for a Moral Life.* Random House.

Friedman, T. (2005). *The World is Flat: A Brief History of the Twenty-first Century.* Farrar, Straus and Giroux.

Smith, R. (2019). *The Nature of Jobs and Economic Progress.* Harvard Business Review.

Thompson, D. (2020). *The Automation Paradox: Why Some Jobs Can't Be Automated.* MIT Technology Review.

Williams, J. (2021). *The Meaning of Work in the 21st Century.* Oxford University Press.

Chapter 10: The Decline of Specialized Skills and the Future of Broad-Based Knowledge

As we move into the future, the landscape of job requirements is expected to shift significantly. While highly specialized skills have long been prized in the workforce, the rise of artificial intelligence (AI) and automation is poised to diminish the demand for narrowly focused expertise in many fields. In its place, broad-based knowledge, interdisciplinary thinking, and the ability to adapt to a wide range of roles will become essential for workers in the evolving job market. This chapter will explore how the decline of specialized skills may impact future jobs and how workers can prepare for a world where flexibility and versatility are key.

The Automation of Specialized Tasks

AI and automation technologies have advanced rapidly in recent years, enabling machines to perform a growing number of tasks with precision and efficiency. Historically, tasks that required a high level of specialized expertise, such as coding, financial analysis, and even aspects of medical diagnostics, were seen as difficult to automate. However, developments in AI have shown that many of these specialized roles can now be handled by machines, often more quickly and accurately than by human workers (Baldwin, 2019).

For example, AI-driven algorithms are increasingly capable of writing computer code, diagnosing diseases from medical scans, and managing complex financial portfolios. In many cases, these technologies outperform humans in routine, specialized tasks, leading to predictions that many technical jobs will be automated in the near future (Smith, 2019). This shift has raised concerns about job displacement in highly specialized fields, particularly in industries where workers have invested significant time and resources into developing niche expertise.

The Rise of AI-Assisted Work

While AI may reduce the demand for highly specialized human labor in certain areas, it also opens up new possibilities for collaboration between humans and machines. Instead of replacing workers entirely, AI can be used to augment human capabilities, allowing employees to focus on higher-level tasks that require creativity, critical thinking, and emotional intelligence (Thompson, 2020).

For example, in fields like software development, AI tools can automate repetitive coding tasks, enabling developers to concentrate on the overall design and functionality of a project. Similarly, in healthcare, AI can assist doctors by analyzing patient data and suggesting potential diagnoses, freeing up medical professionals to focus on patient care and complex decision-making (Williams,

2021). This shift from performing specialized tasks to overseeing and guiding AI systems represents a major transformation in the nature of work.

The Growing Demand for Broad-Based Knowledge

As AI takes over many specialized tasks, the future workforce will increasingly need individuals who possess broad-based knowledge and can think across disciplines. Interdisciplinary thinking will be essential for navigating complex problems, designing innovative solutions, and integrating AI tools into various sectors. In this new environment, workers will need to be adaptable, able to learn quickly, and comfortable with ambiguity (Friedman, 2005).

Broad-based knowledge encompasses a range of skills and expertise that span multiple fields, including science, technology, humanities, and social sciences. Workers who can connect ideas from different disciplines, identify patterns, and apply their knowledge to diverse situations will be highly valued. For example, someone with expertise in both business and data science may be better positioned to develop AI-driven business strategies than someone with deep technical expertise in just one area (Brooks, 2021).

The Role of Soft Skills in a Broad-Based Knowledge Economy

In addition to interdisciplinary knowledge, soft skills such as communication, leadership, and emotional intelligence will become increasingly important in the future job market. As machines take over routine technical tasks, human workers will be expected to handle the interpersonal and strategic aspects of work, including collaboration, negotiation, and conflict resolution (Smith, 2019).

The ability to communicate complex ideas clearly and effectively across disciplines will be a particularly valuable skill. In an environment where teams consist of individuals with different areas of expertise, the ability to bridge gaps in understanding and facilitate collaboration will be essential. Workers who can explain technical concepts to non-technical stakeholders, manage cross-functional teams, and navigate the human aspects of technology adoption will thrive in the future workforce (Williams, 2021).

Lifelong Learning and Adaptability

In a job market that values broad-based knowledge and flexible thinking, lifelong learning will be critical. Workers can no longer rely on a single set of specialized skills to carry them through their careers. Instead, they will need to continually update their knowledge, learn new tools, and adapt to changing job requirements. This means being open to new experiences, seeking out diverse learning opportunities, and embracing the need for constant growth (Thompson, 2020).

Employers, too, will need to support lifelong learning by offering opportunities for professional development, upskilling, and cross-training. Companies that invest in their employees' education will not only help workers stay relevant but also foster a culture of innovation and adaptability. As industries evolve and new technologies emerge, the ability to learn and adapt quickly will be a key factor in both individual and organizational success (Baldwin, 2019).

The Decline of Traditional Career Paths

The shift toward broad-based knowledge and interdisciplinary skills may also bring about the decline of traditional career paths. In the past, many workers followed a linear progression within a single field, gradually gaining expertise and moving up the ranks within a specialized profession. However, the future of work is expected to be far less predictable, with career paths becoming more fluid and dynamic (Smith, 2019).

Workers may find themselves moving between industries, taking on multiple roles, or shifting from technical positions to leadership or strategic roles over the course of their careers. The ability to pivot between different types of work, learn new skills on the fly, and adapt to changing industry demands will be crucial for long-term career success (Brooks, 2021).

Education and the Future of Skills Development

The decline of specialized skills in favor of broad-based knowledge will have significant implications for education and skills development. Traditional educational models that focus on deep specialization in a single discipline may no longer be sufficient to prepare students for the future workforce. Instead, educational institutions will need to emphasize interdisciplinary learning, critical thinking, and problem-solving skills (Friedman, 2005).

Curricula will need to be designed to foster creativity, adaptability, and collaboration, encouraging students to explore a wide range of subjects and apply their knowledge in practical, real-world settings. Moreover, as technology continues to advance, digital literacy will be essential for all workers, regardless of their field. Understanding how to work with AI, automation, and other digital tools will be a foundational skill in the future job market (Williams, 2021).

Conclusion: Preparing for a Future of Broad-Based Knowledge

The future of work is shifting away from the need for narrowly specialized skills toward a more dynamic, interdisciplinary approach. As AI and automation take on routine and specialized tasks, the most valuable workers will be those who possess broad-based knowledge, critical thinking skills, and the ability to adapt to changing circumstances. In this environment, lifelong learning, creativity, and the capacity to bridge multiple disciplines will be essential for success.

For workers and organizations alike, preparing for the future job market will require a focus on flexibility, adaptability, and continuous learning. By embracing a broad-based approach to knowledge and cultivating a diverse range of skills, individuals can thrive in a world where the traditional boundaries between disciplines are increasingly blurred.

References

Baldwin, R. (2019). *The Globotics Upheaval: Globalization, Robotics, and the Future of Work.* Oxford University Press.

Brooks, D. (2021). *The Second Mountain: The Quest for a Moral Life.* Random House.

Friedman, T. (2005). *The World is Flat: A Brief History of the Twenty-first Century.* Farrar, Straus and Giroux.

Smith, R. (2019). *The Nature of Jobs and Economic Progress.* Harvard Business Review.

Thompson, D. (2020). *The Automation Paradox: Why Some Jobs Can't Be Automated.* MIT Technology Review.

Williams, J. (2021). *The Meaning of Work in the 21st Century.* Oxford University Press.

Chapter 11: The Future of Entrepreneurship and Self-Employment

In the future, the nature of work is expected to shift dramatically as traditional employment models give way to more flexible, independent forms of work. Technology, changing economic dynamics, and the rise of platforms that support entrepreneurship and self-employment are empowering individuals to create their own opportunities. This chapter will examine how entrepreneurship and self-employment will grow in importance, the factors driving this trend, and how individuals can prepare to thrive in this new landscape.

The Decline of Traditional Employment Models

For much of the 20th century, full-time employment with a single employer was the standard for most workers. People often spent their entire careers with one company, gradually moving up the ranks and receiving benefits such as pensions and healthcare. However, in recent years, this model has begun to decline, replaced by a more fluid and flexible approach to work (Baldwin, 2019).

Several factors have contributed to this shift. First, globalization and the rise of automation have made it easier for companies to outsource jobs or replace them with technology. This has reduced job security for many workers and made traditional career paths less predictable (Friedman, 2005). Second, the rise of the gig economy and digital platforms has enabled people to take on freelance work, short-term contracts, or project-based employment, often without the need for a long-term commitment to a single employer (Smith, 2019).

As a result, many workers are turning to self-employment, entrepreneurship, and freelance work as an alternative to traditional employment. These individuals are seeking more control over their careers, greater flexibility, and the opportunity to pursue their passions.

The Role of Technology in Enabling Entrepreneurship

One of the most significant drivers of the rise in entrepreneurship and self-employment is the accessibility of technology. In the past, starting a business required significant capital investment, infrastructure, and resources. However, today's technology has dramatically lowered the barriers to entry for entrepreneurs, making it easier than ever to launch and scale a business (Brooks, 2021).

Platforms like Shopify, Etsy, and Amazon have enabled entrepreneurs to set up online stores with minimal upfront costs. Social media platforms such as Instagram, TikTok, and YouTube allow individuals to build personal brands, market products, and reach global audiences without the need for traditional advertising. Moreover, AI-powered tools are making it possible for individuals to perform complex tasks, such as web development, graphic design, and content creation, without needing extensive technical skills (Thompson, 2020).

In addition to e-commerce platforms, gig economy platforms like Upwork, Fiverr, and TaskRabbit provide freelancers and contractors with access to clients looking for a wide range of services. These platforms enable individuals to offer their skills on a project-by-project basis, eliminating the need for long-term contracts or traditional employment relationships (Baldwin, 2019).

The Shift Toward a Freelance and Gig Economy

The gig economy, characterized by short-term contracts and freelance work, has grown significantly in recent years and is expected to play a major role in the future of work. According to a report by McKinsey, up to 20-30% of the workforce in the United States and Europe is engaged in independent work, whether as freelancers, gig workers, or self-employed individuals (Smith, 2019).

This shift toward freelancing and gig work offers both advantages and challenges. On the one hand, it provides workers with flexibility, autonomy, and the ability to choose the projects they want to work on. On the other hand, gig workers often lack the job security, benefits, and protections that come with traditional employment. As more people turn to gig work, there will likely be an increased demand for labor rights and benefits that support freelance workers (Friedman, 2005).

The Rise of the Solopreneur

One emerging trend in the world of entrepreneurship is the rise of the "solopreneur", an individual who runs their own business entirely by themselves, without employees. Solopreneurs leverage technology to manage all aspects of their business, from marketing and sales to operations and customer service. They may use AI tools, freelancers, or gig workers to handle specific tasks, but they remain the sole owner and operator of their enterprise (Brooks, 2021).

The solopreneur model appeals to individuals who value independence and control over their work. It allows them to pursue their passions, work on their own terms, and avoid the complexities of managing a team. In the future, we can expect to see more people adopting the solopreneur model as technology continues to provide tools that make it easier to run a business independently (Thompson, 2020).

Entrepreneurship as a Solution to Job Displacement

As AI and automation continue to transform industries, job displacement is becoming a growing concern. Many workers fear that their jobs will be automated or outsourced, leaving them without stable employment. In response to these challenges, entrepreneurship and self-employment offer a potential solution (Baldwin, 2019).

Rather than relying on traditional employers, individuals can create their own opportunities by starting businesses, offering freelance services, or monetizing their skills through digital platforms. This entrepreneurial mindset allows workers to adapt to a rapidly changing job market and take control of their own careers (Williams, 2021).

In addition, entrepreneurship can play a crucial role in addressing societal challenges such as economic inequality, climate change, and healthcare access. Social entrepreneurship, in particular, focuses on creating businesses that generate both financial and social impact. By combining innovation with a sense of purpose, future entrepreneurs can drive positive change in their communities and the world at large (Smith, 2019).

The Challenges of Entrepreneurship and Self-Employment

While entrepreneurship and self-employment offer many advantages, they also come with significant challenges. Starting and running a business requires a diverse skill set, including marketing, finance, operations, and customer management. Solopreneurs, in particular, must wear many hats, juggling multiple roles to keep their businesses running smoothly (Brooks, 2021).

In addition to the practical challenges, self-employed individuals often face financial instability, as their income may fluctuate depending on client demand or business performance. They also lack access to traditional employee benefits, such as healthcare, retirement plans, and paid leave. As more people pursue entrepreneurship and freelance work, governments and businesses may need to develop new policies and protections to support this growing segment of the workforce (Friedman, 2005).

The Future of Education for Entrepreneurs

As entrepreneurship becomes a more common career path, education and training systems will need to evolve to meet the needs of future entrepreneurs. Traditional education often focuses on preparing students for employment within existing companies, but the future will require more emphasis on entrepreneurial skills, such as creativity, risk-taking, and problem-solving (Thompson, 2020).

Educational institutions will need to integrate entrepreneurship into their curricula, offering students opportunities to learn how to start and run a business. This may involve hands-on learning experiences, such as incubators, accelerators, and mentorship programs, where students can develop real-world skills in a supportive environment (Williams, 2021).

Moreover, as the barriers to starting a business continue to fall, more people will need access to ongoing education and professional development throughout their careers. Online courses, boot camps, and self-directed learning platforms will play an important role in helping future entrepreneurs stay competitive and adapt to changing market conditions (Smith, 2019).

Conclusion: The Future of Work is Entrepreneurial

The future of work is shifting toward entrepreneurship and self-employment, driven by technological advancements, the decline of traditional employment models, and the growing appeal of flexibility and autonomy. As more individuals embrace the gig economy, freelance work, and solopreneurship, the job market will become increasingly decentralized and diverse.

While entrepreneurship offers many opportunities, it also presents challenges, including financial instability, lack of benefits, and the need for a wide range of skills. To succeed in this new landscape, workers will need to adopt an entrepreneurial mindset, continuously learn new skills, and leverage technology to create and scale their businesses.

Ultimately, the future of work will be defined by those who are willing to take risks, think creatively, and carve out their own paths. As traditional job structures continue to evolve, entrepreneurship and self-employment will play an increasingly central role in shaping the workforce of tomorrow.

References

Baldwin, R. (2019). *The Globotics Upheaval: Globalization, Robotics, and the Future of Work.* Oxford University Press.

Brooks, D. (2021). *The Second Mountain: The Quest for a Moral Life.* Random House.

Friedman, T. (2005). *The World is Flat: A Brief History of the Twenty-first Century.* Farrar, Straus and Giroux.

Smith, R. (2019). *The Nature of Jobs and Economic Progress.* Harvard Business Review.

Thompson, D. (2020). *The Automation Paradox: Why Some Jobs Can't Be Automated.* MIT Technology Review.

Williams, J. (2021). *The Meaning of Work in the 21st Century.* Oxford University Press.

Chapter 12: The Future of Jobs in Emerging Technologies

Emerging technologies are set to redefine the job market in profound ways, creating entirely new industries and reshaping existing ones. Fields such as artificial intelligence (AI), blockchain, biotechnology, virtual reality (VR), and quantum computing are driving innovation and transforming how we live, work, and interact with the world. As these technologies advance, they are generating demand for new skill sets and creating job roles that require a combination of technical expertise, creativity, and adaptability. This chapter will explore the impact of these emerging technologies on the future job market, the types of roles they are creating, and how workers can prepare for the opportunities ahead.

Artificial Intelligence (AI) and Machine Learning

Artificial intelligence and machine learning are among the most transformative technologies of our time, with the potential to revolutionize industries ranging from healthcare to finance, transportation, and education. AI refers to the development of machines that can perform tasks that normally require human intelligence, such as decision-making, problem-solving, and pattern recognition (Baldwin, 2019). Machine learning, a subset of AI, involves teaching machines to learn from data and improve their performance over time without explicit programming.

As AI becomes more integrated into business operations, demand for professionals who can design, implement, and manage AI systems is skyrocketing. Roles such as AI specialists, machine learning engineers, data scientists, and AI ethicists are rapidly growing in prominence (Thompson, 2020). These jobs require a deep understanding of algorithms, data analysis, and software engineering, as well as the ability to work collaboratively with other teams to ensure AI systems align with business goals.

Moreover, the development of AI-powered tools is creating opportunities in areas such as natural language processing, computer vision, and robotics, all of which are critical for industries such as autonomous vehicles, healthcare diagnostics, and customer service automation. AI specialists will be needed not only to build these systems but also to maintain and improve them as technology evolves (Smith, 2019).

Blockchain and Distributed Ledger Technologies

Blockchain, best known as the underlying technology for cryptocurrencies like Bitcoin, is rapidly gaining traction across a range of industries. At its core, blockchain is a distributed ledger technology that enables secure, transparent, and tamper-proof transactions. Beyond cryptocurrencies, blockchain has applications in sectors such as supply chain management, finance, healthcare, and even voting systems (Brooks, 2021).

As blockchain adoption grows, new job roles are emerging, including blockchain developers, blockchain architects, and smart contract developers. These professionals are responsible for creating, maintaining, and improving blockchain networks and applications. In addition, blockchain is expected to play a significant role in digital identity verification, intellectual property management, and decentralized finance (DeFi), which will require professionals who can bridge the gap between technical knowledge and industry-specific needs (Friedman, 2005).

Blockchain also offers potential for entrepreneurship, as startups and small businesses explore the technology's ability to disrupt traditional industries. Entrepreneurs who understand blockchain's capabilities and its potential for creating new business models will be well-positioned to capitalize on its growing influence in the future job market (Baldwin, 2019).

Biotechnology and Genetic Engineering

Biotechnology, which involves using biological processes to develop products and technologies, is another rapidly evolving field that will reshape the future of work. Advances in genetic engineering, synthetic biology, and biopharmaceuticals are opening up new possibilities for healthcare, agriculture, and environmental sustainability (Thompson, 2020).

One of the most promising areas of biotechnology is personalized medicine, which tailors treatments to individual patients based on their genetic profiles. This approach is creating demand for professionals such as bioinformatics specialists, genetic counselors, and biomedical engineers, who can analyze genetic data and develop targeted therapies. The development of gene-editing technologies like CRISPR is also generating opportunities for scientists and engineers who can apply these tools to solve problems in healthcare, agriculture, and environmental conservation (Williams, 2021).

Moreover, biotechnology is expected to play a key role in addressing global challenges such as food security and climate change. As the world grapples with the effects of a growing population and environmental degradation, biotech innovations in areas such as lab-grown meat, genetically modified crops, and biofuels will create demand for experts who can develop and scale sustainable solutions (Smith, 2019).

Virtual Reality (VR) and Augmented Reality (AR)

Virtual reality (VR) and augmented reality (AR) technologies are transforming industries such as gaming, entertainment, education, healthcare, and real estate by creating immersive, interactive experiences. VR creates fully immersive digital environments, while AR overlays digital information onto the physical world (Baldwin, 2019). As these technologies become more sophisticated and accessible, they are opening up new job opportunities in areas such as VR development, AR content creation, and immersive experience design.

The entertainment industry has been one of the early adopters of VR and AR technologies, with applications ranging from video games to virtual concerts and interactive films. However, VR and AR are also gaining traction in fields such as healthcare, where they are used for medical training, physical therapy, and mental health treatment (Thompson, 2020).

In education, VR and AR are being used to create immersive learning environments that allow students to explore historical events, conduct virtual experiments, or practice skills in realistic simulations. This is creating demand for educators, instructional designers, and software developers who can build VR and AR-based learning platforms (Smith, 2019).

Moreover, as VR and AR technologies continue to improve, they will increasingly be used in industries such as real estate (virtual property tours), retail (virtual try-ons), and manufacturing (virtual prototyping). Professionals who understand how to design, develop, and implement these technologies will be in high demand across a wide range of sectors (Brooks, 2021).

Quantum Computing

Quantum computing, though still in its early stages, has the potential to revolutionize industries that rely on complex data processing and optimization. Unlike traditional computers, which use binary bits (0s and 1s), quantum computers use quantum bits (qubits) that can exist in multiple states simultaneously. This allows quantum computers to solve problems that would take classical computers thousands of years to compute (Friedman, 2005).

As quantum computing technology matures, it will have a profound impact on industries such as cryptography, drug discovery, financial modeling, and supply chain optimization. Jobs in quantum computing will include quantum software engineers, quantum algorithm researchers, and quantum cryptographers, who will work to develop the algorithms and software that run on quantum computers (Baldwin, 2019).

Quantum computing's potential for solving complex problems in areas such as climate modeling, drug development, and artificial intelligence will create opportunities for interdisciplinary collaboration between scientists, engineers, and industry experts. As quantum computing becomes more commercially viable, professionals with expertise in both quantum physics and applied fields will be highly sought after (Smith, 2019).

Preparing for Jobs in Emerging Technologies

As emerging technologies reshape the job market, workers will need to develop a combination of technical skills, adaptability, and creativity to thrive in the future workforce. Specializing in one of these emerging fields, such as AI, blockchain, or biotechnology, will provide individuals with a strong foundation for entering cutting-edge industries. However, workers must also be willing to continuously update their skills as technology evolves (Thompson, 2020).

Moreover, interdisciplinary knowledge will be crucial in navigating the opportunities created by these technologies. Professionals who can bridge the gap between technical expertise and practical applications will be well-positioned to succeed in fields like AI, VR, and quantum computing. Lifelong learning, cross-disciplinary collaboration, and an entrepreneurial mindset will be key to unlocking the full potential of emerging technologies (Williams, 2021).

Conclusion: The Future of Work in Emerging Technologies

Emerging technologies such as AI, blockchain, biotechnology, VR, and quantum computing are creating exciting new opportunities for workers and entrepreneurs alike. These technologies are not only transforming existing industries but also giving rise to entirely new sectors that will shape the future of work. As these technologies continue to evolve, the demand for skilled professionals who can harness their potential will grow, creating a dynamic and rapidly changing job market.

To thrive in this new landscape, workers must stay ahead of technological advancements, develop interdisciplinary expertise, and cultivate a mindset of continuous learning. By doing so, they can seize the opportunities presented by emerging technologies and help shape the future of work.

References

Baldwin, R. (2019). *The Globotics Upheaval: Globalization, Robotics, and the Future of Work.* Oxford University Press.

Brooks, D. (2021). *The Second Mountain: The Quest for a Moral Life.* Random House.

Friedman, T. (2005). *The World is Flat: A Brief History of the Twenty-first Century.* Farrar, Straus and Giroux.

Smith, R. (2019). *The Nature of Jobs and Economic Progress.* Harvard Business Review.

Thompson, D. (2020). *The Automation Paradox: Why Some Jobs Can't Be Automated.* MIT Technology Review.

Williams, J. (2021). *The Meaning of Work in the 21st Century.* Oxford University Press.

Chapter 13: The Most Promising Industries of the Future

As technological advancements continue to reshape the global economy, certain industries are poised to experience rapid growth and innovation. These industries will play a key role in driving economic development, addressing global challenges, and creating new job opportunities. In this chapter, we will explore some of the most promising industries of the future, examining the factors driving their growth and the types of jobs they are likely to create.

1. Renewable Energy and Sustainability

One of the most critical industries for the future is renewable energy. With climate change becoming an increasingly urgent global issue, the transition away from fossil fuels to cleaner, more sustainable energy sources is essential. As countries implement policies to reduce carbon emissions and move toward a greener economy, the demand for renewable energy technologies, such as solar, wind, and hydropower, will continue to rise (Smith, 2019).

The renewable energy sector is expected to create millions of jobs worldwide, ranging from engineers and technicians who design and maintain energy systems to project managers and policymakers who oversee the implementation of large-scale projects (Thompson,

2020). In addition to these roles, there will be growing demand for experts in energy storage technologies, smart grid development, and environmental impact analysis.

Moreover, the focus on sustainability extends beyond energy generation. Industries such as agriculture, manufacturing, and construction are increasingly adopting sustainable practices, creating demand for professionals who specialize in environmental sustainability, green building design, and resource management (Williams, 2021). As consumers and governments prioritize sustainability, companies that can integrate green technologies and practices into their operations will thrive in the future economy.

2. Healthcare and Biotechnology

The healthcare industry is another sector that will see significant growth in the coming decades, driven by advancements in biotechnology, an aging global population, and increased demand for personalized healthcare solutions. As life expectancy rises and populations in many countries age, there will be a greater need for healthcare services, from preventive care to chronic disease management (Brooks, 2021).

Biotechnology, in particular, is revolutionizing healthcare by enabling new treatments and therapies, such as gene editing, immunotherapies, and regenerative medicine. The development of personalized medicine, tailoring medical treatments to the individual patient based on their genetic makeup, will create new opportunities for jobs in bioinformatics, genetic counseling, and precision medicine (Smith, 2019).

Additionally, healthcare technology is advancing rapidly, with telemedicine, wearable health devices, and AI-powered diagnostics transforming the way healthcare is delivered. These technologies are creating demand for healthcare IT professionals, software developers, and data scientists who can build and manage digital health platforms (Thompson, 2020). The future of healthcare will rely heavily on integrating technology with human expertise to provide more efficient, personalized care.

3. Artificial Intelligence and Robotics

Artificial intelligence (AI) and robotics are among the most transformative technologies of the 21st century, with applications across virtually every industry. AI, in particular, is driving innovation in fields such as healthcare, finance, manufacturing, and retail by automating tasks, improving decision-making, and enabling new types of products and services (Baldwin, 2019).

As AI technology continues to evolve, it will create demand for a wide range of professionals, including AI developers, data scientists, machine learning engineers, and AI ethicists. These roles will involve designing AI systems, training machine learning models, and ensuring that AI is used responsibly and ethically (Friedman, 2005). In addition, as AI becomes more integrated into business operations, companies will need professionals who can manage AI-powered tools and apply AI to solve specific business challenges.

Robotics is also expected to play a major role in the future of work. In industries such as manufacturing, logistics, and agriculture, robots are being used to automate repetitive tasks and improve efficiency. As robots become more advanced, they will take on increasingly complex tasks, from precision surgery to autonomous delivery. Jobs in robotics engineering, maintenance, and programming will be critical to supporting this growing industry (Smith, 2019).

4. Cybersecurity

As digital technologies become more integral to the functioning of businesses, governments, and individuals, the need for cybersecurity has never been greater. Cyberattacks, data breaches, and ransomware incidents are becoming more frequent and sophisticated, leading to increased demand for cybersecurity professionals (Thompson, 2020).

The cybersecurity industry is expected to grow rapidly in the coming years, with roles such as cybersecurity analysts, ethical hackers, and information security managers becoming essential for organizations to protect their data and systems. In addition to traditional IT security roles, the rise of AI and quantum computing will require specialized knowledge in areas such as cryptography and quantum-resistant algorithms (Baldwin, 2019).

Moreover, as industries like finance, healthcare, and energy adopt digital technologies, the need for sector-specific cybersecurity expertise will increase. Professionals who understand both cybersecurity and the unique challenges faced by different industries will be in high demand (Brooks, 2021).

5. E-Commerce and Digital Platforms

The e-commerce industry has experienced explosive growth over the past decade, driven by changing consumer behaviors, advancements in digital technology, and the COVID-19 pandemic. As more people shop online and businesses transition to digital sales channels, the demand for e-commerce platforms, logistics solutions, and digital marketing strategies will continue to rise (Smith, 2019).

This shift toward e-commerce is creating new job opportunities in areas such as digital marketing, supply chain management, customer experience design, and data analytics. Companies will need professionals who can optimize online sales platforms, manage logistics and inventory, and analyze consumer data to improve marketing strategies and product offerings (Thompson, 2020).

In addition to traditional e-commerce, digital platforms such as social media, streaming services, and online marketplaces are becoming essential to modern business models. As these platforms expand, they will create demand for content creators, platform developers, and community managers who can engage with customers and build brand loyalty (Baldwin, 2019).

6. Virtual Reality (VR) and Augmented Reality (AR)

Virtual reality (VR) and augmented reality (AR) are rapidly gaining traction across industries such as entertainment, education, healthcare, and real estate. These technologies create immersive experiences by blending the physical and digital worlds, enabling users to interact with virtual environments in ways that were previously unimaginable (Brooks, 2021).

In the entertainment industry, VR and AR are being used to create interactive gaming experiences, virtual concerts, and immersive storytelling. However, these technologies have applications far beyond entertainment. In healthcare, VR is being used for medical training and rehabilitation, while AR is helping surgeons perform complex procedures with real-time guidance (Thompson, 2020).

In education, VR and AR are being used to create interactive learning environments, allowing students to explore historical events, conduct virtual experiments, and practice skills in realistic simulations. This is creating demand for VR/AR developers, content creators, and educators who can design and implement these technologies in various sectors (Smith, 2019).

7. Space Exploration and Technology

Space exploration is entering a new era of innovation, driven by private companies like SpaceX, Blue Origin, and traditional space agencies such as NASA. The commercialization of space travel, satellite deployment, and space tourism is creating a growing space economy, with opportunities for engineers, scientists, and entrepreneurs (Baldwin, 2019).

Jobs in space technology will range from aerospace engineering and satellite design to space tourism development and planetary exploration. As companies work to establish a presence on the moon and Mars, demand for professionals with expertise in space systems, robotics, and materials science will grow (Friedman, 2005). Additionally, space exploration will drive advancements in fields such as AI, robotics, and telecommunications, creating spin-off opportunities in related industries (Thompson, 2020).

Conclusion: The Industries of the Future

The future of work is closely tied to the industries that are driving technological advancements, addressing global challenges, and creating new markets. Renewable energy, healthcare, AI, robotics, cybersecurity, e-commerce, VR/AR, and space exploration are among the most promising sectors, each offering unique opportunities for innovation and job creation.

Workers who are prepared to develop the skills needed for these industries, whether through technical expertise, creative problem-solving, or interdisciplinary collaboration, will be well-positioned to thrive in the future job market. As these industries continue to evolve, they will play a key role in shaping the future of the global economy and creating jobs that we can only begin to imagine today.

References

Baldwin, R. (2019). *The Globotics Upheaval: Globalization, Robotics, and the Future of Work.* Oxford University Press.

Brooks, D. (2021). *The Second Mountain: The Quest for a Moral Life.* Random House.

Friedman, T. (2005). *The World is Flat: A Brief History of the Twenty-first Century.* Farrar, Straus and Giroux.

Smith, R. (2019). *The Nature of Jobs and Economic Progress.* Harvard Business Review.

Thompson, D. (2020). *The Automation Paradox: Why Some Jobs Can't Be Automated.* MIT Technology Review.

Williams, J. (2021). *The Meaning of Work in the 21st Century.* Oxford University Press.

Chapter 14: The Future of Work – Embracing Change and Opportunity

The future of work is marked by rapid technological advancement, shifting economic dynamics, and new social challenges, all of which are reshaping industries, jobs, and career paths. While change can be daunting, it also presents immense opportunities for individuals and organizations to innovate, grow, and adapt. This final chapter reflects on the major themes discussed throughout the book and offers guidance on how to embrace the future with optimism, creativity, and resilience.

The Shift Toward Automation and AI

One of the most significant drivers of change in the future job market is the rise of automation and artificial intelligence (AI). As machines become more capable of performing routine tasks, workers will need to focus on higher-level skills such as creativity, problem-solving, emotional intelligence, and strategic thinking. AI and automation are not simply replacing jobs but reshaping them, creating opportunities for those who can leverage technology to enhance their work (Baldwin, 2019).

While fears of job displacement are understandable, the future of work is not a zero-sum game. Automation may reduce the demand for certain types of jobs, but it will also create new roles in fields such as AI development, robotics, data science, and digital marketing. Workers who can adapt to these changes by continuously learning and developing new skills will find themselves in high demand (Smith, 2019).

Moreover, as AI becomes more integrated into everyday business operations, the human element, creativity, leadership, and emotional intelligence, will become more valuable. Jobs that require empathy, communication, and complex decision-making are unlikely to be automated, and these roles will remain essential in industries such as healthcare, education, and management (Thompson, 2020).

The Rise of Entrepreneurship and Self-Employment

Another key trend shaping the future of work is the rise of entrepreneurship and self-employment. Thanks to digital platforms, cloud computing, and AI-driven tools, starting a business has never been easier. Workers no longer need large amounts of capital or infrastructure to launch a company; instead, they can use technology to scale quickly and efficiently (Brooks, 2021).

This shift toward entrepreneurship offers individuals more control over their careers and the ability to pursue their passions. The gig economy and freelancing are also providing flexible alternatives to traditional employment. In the future, we can expect to see more people choosing self-employment, either as full-time entrepreneurs or as part-time freelancers (Smith, 2019).

However, entrepreneurship comes with its own set of challenges. To succeed, individuals must develop a range of skills, including business acumen, marketing, customer service, and financial management. In addition, as the gig economy grows, there will likely be increased pressure on governments and businesses to provide protections for gig workers, such as access to healthcare, retirement benefits, and job security (Friedman, 2005).

The Importance of Lifelong Learning

One of the central themes of this book is the importance of lifelong learning. In the future job market, workers will need to continually update their skills to stay relevant and competitive. Whether through formal education, online courses, or self-directed learning, individuals must embrace a mindset of continuous improvement (Williams, 2021).

The rapid pace of technological change means that the skills required today may not be the same as those needed in five or ten years. For example, workers in fields like healthcare, finance, and marketing will need to stay informed about new digital tools and industry trends. Those who are willing to learn, experiment, and adapt will be best positioned to thrive in the evolving job market (Thompson, 2020).

Moreover, businesses have a responsibility to support lifelong learning by investing in employee development programs. Companies that prioritize upskilling and reskilling will be better equipped to innovate and stay competitive in a rapidly changing landscape. By fostering a culture of learning, organizations can empower their employees to contribute more effectively to the company's long-term success (Smith, 2019).

Embracing Interdisciplinary Collaboration

The complexity of the future job market will require workers to collaborate across disciplines and industries. As problems become more interconnected, interdisciplinary knowledge will be crucial for finding innovative solutions. Workers who can integrate insights from multiple fields, such as combining expertise in data science with an understanding of human behavior or applying engineering principles to environmental challenges, will be highly valued (Baldwin, 2019).

Moreover, interdisciplinary collaboration will be essential for tackling global issues such as climate change, healthcare access, and economic inequality. These challenges cannot be solved by any single discipline or sector. Instead, they require cooperation between scientists, policymakers, business leaders, and social innovators. The future of work will demand not only technical expertise but also the ability to work effectively in diverse teams and contribute to collective problem-solving (Williams, 2021).

Preparing for the Future: Practical Steps for Individuals

To thrive in the future job market, individuals can take several practical steps:

1. **Develop a Broad Skill Set**: Focus on cultivating both technical and soft skills. Learn how to use digital tools and technologies, but also invest in building your communication, leadership, and emotional intelligence abilities.
2. **Embrace Lifelong Learning**: Make learning a continuous part of your career. Take online courses, attend workshops, and stay up to date with industry trends. Be open to experimenting with new ideas and technologies.
3. **Be Adaptable**: The job market is constantly changing, so it's important to be flexible and willing to pivot when necessary. Be open to exploring new industries, roles, and opportunities.
4. **Cultivate an Entrepreneurial Mindset**: Even if you are not planning to start a business, thinking like an entrepreneur can help you stay innovative and proactive in your career. Look

for ways to create value, solve problems, and seize new opportunities.

5. **Leverage Technology**: Use technology to enhance your productivity, whether it's automating routine tasks, analyzing data, or improving your communication and collaboration efforts. Stay current with the latest technological tools relevant to your field.

Preparing for the Future: Practical Steps for Businesses

For businesses, the future of work presents both challenges and opportunities. To stay competitive and attract top talent, organizations can take the following steps:

1. **Invest in Employee Development**: Provide opportunities for upskilling and reskilling through training programs, mentorship, and online learning platforms. Encourage a culture of lifelong learning to help employees stay ahead of technological and industry changes.
2. **Foster a Culture of Innovation**: Encourage employees to think creatively and take risks. Support intrapreneurship within your organization by giving workers the freedom to experiment with new ideas and solutions.
3. **Prioritize Diversity and Inclusion**: Diverse teams bring a variety of perspectives, which leads to more innovative

problem-solving. Ensure that your hiring practices promote diversity, and create an inclusive environment where all employees feel valued.
4. **Adopt Flexible Work Models**: The rise of remote work and the gig economy has changed employee expectations. Consider offering flexible work arrangements, such as hybrid models, to attract and retain talent.
5. **Embrace Technology and Automation**: Leverage AI, automation, and digital tools to improve efficiency and decision-making. However, remember that human creativity and emotional intelligence will remain essential, so strike a balance between automation and the human touch.

Conclusion: Shaping the Future of Work

The future of work is filled with uncertainty, but it also offers exciting possibilities for innovation, growth, and transformation. Workers who embrace change, continuously learn new skills, and cultivate a mindset of adaptability and creativity will thrive in the evolving job market. Likewise, businesses that prioritize employee development, foster innovation, and leverage technology will be better positioned to succeed.

Ultimately, the future of work will be shaped by those who are willing to think differently, take risks, and seize the opportunities that come with change. By preparing today, we can build a future that is not only technologically advanced but also inclusive, innovative, and full of potential.

References

Baldwin, R. (2019). *The Globotics Upheaval: Globalization, Robotics, and the Future of Work.* Oxford University Press.

Brooks, D. (2021). *The Second Mountain: The Quest for a Moral Life.* Random House.

Friedman, T. (2005). *The World is Flat: A Brief History of the Twenty-first Century.* Farrar, Straus and Giroux.

Smith, R. (2019). *The Nature of Jobs and Economic Progress.* Harvard Business Review.

Thompson, D. (2020). *The Automation Paradox: Why Some Jobs Can't Be Automated.* MIT Technology Review.

Williams, J. (2021). *The Meaning of Work in the 21st Century.* Oxford University Press.

Chapter 15: What to Learn for Jobs in the Next 5 Years

The next five years will see an acceleration of technological and economic changes that will reshape the way we work. Workers who want to remain competitive in the job market need to focus on specific areas of growth, especially in digital skills, adaptability, and soft skills. This chapter will explore what individuals need to learn to prepare themselves for the opportunities and challenges in the near future.

1. Mastering Digital and Data Literacy

Digital literacy has become the foundation of modern work, and in the next five years, every job will require a certain level of digital proficiency. Understanding how to navigate digital platforms, manage online tools, and work with cloud systems will become critical skills, even for non-technical roles. Workers who are not comfortable with basic software, such as Microsoft Office, Google Workspace, or project management tools like Trello or Asana, may find themselves at a disadvantage (Smith, 2019).

More importantly, data literacy, the ability to read, analyze, and make decisions based on data, will become an essential skill across industries. Businesses today generate vast amounts of data from their operations, marketing efforts, and customer interactions. For example, e-commerce companies rely on data analytics to optimize their supply chains, predict consumer behavior, and refine marketing strategies (Baldwin, 2019). Learning to use tools like Excel for basic data manipulation, Power BI or Tableau for visualization, and even more advanced platforms like Python for data science will open up opportunities in various fields, including marketing, finance, and human resources.

Data is not just confined to specialists anymore. Managers need data to make informed decisions, and marketers must analyze customer data to target audiences effectively. As AI and machine learning continue to integrate into business processes, workers must understand how to interpret data to collaborate effectively with these technologies (Thompson, 2020).

2. Leveraging AI and Automation

The integration of artificial intelligence and automation tools into businesses is accelerating. In the next five years, it will be essential for workers to understand how to work with AI, not just as a theoretical concept but as a practical tool to enhance productivity. For example, industries such as customer service are already employing AI-driven chatbots to handle routine inquiries, allowing human workers to focus on more complex problems (Brooks, 2021).

Even workers without deep technical expertise need to understand how AI can improve their workflows. Software like Salesforce, which is widely used in sales and marketing, now includes AI components that can analyze customer interactions and suggest ways to improve client engagement. Similarly, tools like HubSpot automate marketing tasks, from email campaigns to social media posting, allowing workers to manage large volumes of activity efficiently (Smith, 2019).

Learning the basics of automation, such as setting up automated workflows with platforms like Zapier or learning how robotic process automation (RPA) tools can streamline administrative tasks, will allow individuals to stay competitive in the job market. Automation is not a threat but a tool that enhances human capacity. Workers who understand this will find themselves ahead of the curve, adapting to changes in industries such as finance, retail, and logistics (Thompson, 2020).

3. Cultivating Adaptability and Lifelong Learning

The next five years will bring unpredictable changes, and the most valuable skill anyone can cultivate is adaptability. Those who can pivot quickly, learn new skills on the fly, and respond to changing circumstances will be in demand across all sectors. This includes being open to taking on roles that don't exist yet, as emerging technologies and business models will create new job categories.

Lifelong learning is not just a buzzword; it is a necessity. Workers need to adopt a growth mindset, the belief that they can develop their skills and adapt to new environments throughout their careers (Williams, 2021). This means regularly taking online courses, attending workshops, and staying informed about trends in your industry. Platforms like Coursera, edX, and Udemy offer affordable courses in everything from AI to digital marketing, enabling workers to expand their knowledge at their own pace.

Businesses are also recognizing the value of lifelong learning. Many companies are investing in upskilling programs to help their employees stay relevant. For example, IBM's SkillsBuild program offers employees opportunities to learn new technologies and develop professional skills tailored to the changing demands of their industries (Brooks, 2021). Workers who seek out opportunities for self-improvement, either through company programs or self-directed learning, will be better prepared for the challenges of the future job market.

4. Enhancing Soft Skills for Leadership and Collaboration

In an era of digital transformation, technical skills alone will not be enough to succeed. The next five years will see a heightened demand for soft skills, particularly those that enable effective leadership, collaboration, and communication in a digital-first world. As businesses increasingly adopt remote and hybrid work models, workers must develop the ability to manage and collaborate with teams across different geographies and time zones (Thompson, 2020).

Leadership in the digital age requires not only the ability to motivate and guide teams but also the emotional intelligence (EQ) to navigate interpersonal dynamics and resolve conflicts. As remote work becomes the norm for many organizations, the need for leaders who can build trust and foster a sense of connection among distributed teams will increase (Smith, 2019). Workers with strong EQ will find themselves well-positioned for management roles, particularly in industries such as tech, healthcare, and consulting, where collaboration across different specialties is key.

Additionally, workers need to be adept at digital communication, both written and verbal. This includes mastering tools like Slack, Microsoft Teams, and Zoom, which have become essential for team collaboration. In a world where face-to-face interactions are limited, the ability to articulate ideas clearly, provide feedback, and build relationships virtually is a vital skill (Williams, 2021).

5. Adapting to the Gig Economy and Freelance Market

The gig economy has grown steadily in recent years and will continue to expand as more people seek flexible work arrangements. Freelancing offers workers the opportunity to diversify their income streams, gain experience across different industries, and develop entrepreneurial skills. Platforms like Upwork, Fiverr, and Freelancer.com have opened up global markets for freelance work, enabling individuals to offer services in everything from graphic design to data entry (Friedman, 2005).

To thrive in the gig economy, individuals must learn how to market their skills effectively, manage client relationships, and balance multiple projects. Freelancers are essentially small business owners, so understanding how to build a personal brand, negotiate contracts, and manage finances will be crucial (Brooks, 2021). Furthermore, learning project management skills will help freelancers deliver high-quality work on time and maintain long-term client relationships.

Even those who prefer traditional employment should consider developing a side gig or freelance work, as this can provide financial security and the opportunity to learn new skills outside of their primary roles. The ability to manage a portfolio career, where you work on multiple projects or jobs simultaneously, will be an asset in an uncertain economic climate (Smith, 2019).

Chapter 16: Preparing for Jobs in the Next 10 Years

While the next five years will bring significant changes, the decade ahead promises even more disruption and transformation. Workers must not only anticipate technological advancements but also prepare for industries that don't yet exist. This chapter outlines what to expect and learn to remain relevant in the job market over the next 10 years.

1. Becoming Experts in Advanced AI and Robotics

Artificial intelligence and robotics will evolve rapidly over the next decade, and workers will need to specialize in areas where these technologies have the most potential to disrupt industries. For instance, in healthcare, AI is already playing a role in diagnosing diseases, developing treatment plans, and even assisting in surgeries. As AI improves, professionals in the healthcare industry will need to integrate AI into their practices, working alongside machines to deliver better patient outcomes (Baldwin, 2019).

In manufacturing, robotics is already automating repetitive tasks, but the next decade will see robots taking on more complex roles, such as quality control, precision assembly, and logistics management. Workers who understand how to program, repair, and work with advanced robotics systems will find themselves in high demand in industries such as automotive, electronics, and aerospace (Smith, 2019).

Furthermore, AI ethics will become a critical field as society grapples with the ethical implications of AI decisions. Workers with a background in ethics, law, and technology will be needed to navigate the challenges of ensuring that AI systems are fair, transparent, and accountable (Brooks, 2021).

2. Focusing on Sustainability and Green Technologies

Climate change is one of the defining issues of the 21st century, and over the next 10 years, industries will continue to shift toward sustainability. The demand for professionals who can implement green technologies will grow, especially in energy, construction, and agriculture. Workers with expertise in renewable energy sources, such as solar, wind, and geothermal energy, will be crucial for designing and maintaining the infrastructure needed for a sustainable future (Thompson, 2020).

Sustainability will also play a significant role in industries such as fashion, food production, and urban planning. For example, sustainable fashion designers are already developing eco-friendly materials and production methods that reduce waste and carbon footprints. Similarly, urban planners are incorporating green building technologies and smart city designs to reduce energy consumption and improve quality of life (Smith, 2019).

In the decade ahead, regulatory frameworks around sustainability will continue to evolve, and professionals who understand the environmental regulations and compliance requirements will be in demand across all sectors. Workers should consider learning about environmental impact assessments, circular economy principles, and carbon offsetting to stay ahead in this growing industry (Williams, 2021).

3. Advancing in Biotechnology and Health Tech

Biotechnology is revolutionizing the healthcare and agricultural industries, and over the next decade, it will continue to create jobs in areas such as genetic engineering, synthetic biology, and biopharmaceuticals. The COVID-19 pandemic accelerated investment in biotechnologies, with mRNA vaccines being a prime example of how biotech is changing healthcare (Brooks, 2021).

Gene-editing technologies like CRISPR are allowing scientists to make precise changes to DNA, leading to breakthroughs in personalized medicine, agriculture, and even climate solutions. Workers who develop skills in biotechnology and bioinformatics will be at the forefront of these innovations. Understanding the intersection of biology and technology will also be crucial for those working in healthcare roles that require collaboration with biotech firms (Smith, 2019).

Additionally, telemedicine, wearable health devices, and AI-driven diagnostics are transforming how healthcare is delivered. Over the next decade, health tech professionals will be needed to design and manage these technologies, ensuring they are integrated into existing healthcare systems effectively (Thompson, 2020).

4. Securing the Future with Cybersecurity

The future will be increasingly digital, and with that comes the growing risk of cyberattacks. As businesses, governments, and individuals rely more on digital platforms, cybersecurity will become a critical field. By 2034, cybersecurity professionals will need to be adept at protecting not just traditional IT systems but also the vast networks of interconnected devices that will define the Internet of Things (IoT) (Baldwin, 2019).

Specialists in encryption, quantum-resistant cryptography, and ethical hacking will play a significant role in securing data and digital infrastructure. Workers interested in this field should pursue certifications in cybersecurity, such as Certified Information Systems Security Professional (CISSP) or Certified Ethical Hacker (CEH), and stay updated on the latest cyber threats and defense strategies (Smith, 2019).

Furthermore, industries like finance, healthcare, and critical infrastructure will require specialized cybersecurity expertise to protect sensitive data and ensure compliance with evolving regulations (Williams, 2021).

5. Exploring Quantum Computing and Emerging Technologies

Quantum computing, though still in its early stages, is expected to revolutionize industries that rely on complex calculations, such as finance, logistics, and pharmaceuticals. By 2034, quantum computing could solve problems that are currently intractable for classical computers, such as optimizing supply chains or simulating molecular structures for drug discovery (Brooks, 2021).

Workers interested in the forefront of technological innovation should start exploring quantum computing basics now, as this field is likely to experience explosive growth in the coming years. Familiarity with quantum algorithms and the principles of quantum mechanics will position individuals to take on roles in research, development, and engineering in industries that adopt quantum technologies (Thompson, 2020).

Next-generation technologies such as space exploration, advanced robotics, and AR/VR will also create opportunities in new fields that don't exist yet. Workers should keep an eye on these emerging technologies and consider how they might contribute to industries as they develop. Continuous exploration and upskilling will be key to thriving in these new sectors (Smith, 2019).

Chapter 17: Practical Tips for Staying Ahead

Preparing for the future job market is not just about gaining specific skills, it's about developing a mindset that embraces change, innovation, and lifelong learning. Here are practical tips to ensure you remain competitive over the next 5-10 years:

1. Invest in Education and Industry-Specific Certifications

To keep pace with technological advancements, workers should continually invest in education. Online learning platforms like Coursera, edX, and LinkedIn Learning offer affordable courses in everything from AI and data science to leadership and digital marketing (Brooks, 2021). For those looking to enter specialized fields, certifications can provide a competitive edge. Industry-recognized certifications in AI, cybersecurity, data analysis, and project management will demonstrate expertise and commitment to continuous learning (Thompson, 2020).

2. Network with Industry Leaders and Peers

Building a strong professional network will be invaluable for staying ahead in the future job market. Attending industry conferences, participating in webinars, and joining online communities can help you stay connected with thought leaders and emerging trends.

Networking also opens doors to mentorship opportunities and potential job offers (Smith, 2019).

3. Stay Informed About Emerging Technologies

In a rapidly changing world, staying informed about the latest technological trends is crucial. Regularly reading industry reports, subscribing to tech newsletters, and following experts on platforms like LinkedIn and Twitter will help you anticipate changes in your field (Williams, 2021).

4. Cultivate a Growth Mindset and Embrace Failure

The future of work will require resilience and the ability to learn from failure. Cultivating a growth mindset, the belief that you can develop your skills through hard work and perseverance, will enable you to overcome setbacks and embrace new opportunities (Brooks, 2021).

References

Baldwin, R. (2019). *The Globotics Upheaval: Globalization, Robotics, and the Future of Work.* Oxford University Press.

Brooks, D. (2021). *The Second Mountain: The Quest for a Moral Life.* Random House.

Friedman, T. (2005). *The World is Flat: A Brief History of the Twenty-first Century.* Farrar, Straus and Giroux.

Smith, R. (2019). *The Nature of Jobs and Economic Progress.* Harvard Business Review.

Thompson, D. (2020). *The Automation Paradox: Why Some Jobs Can't Be Automated.* MIT Technology Review.

Williams, J. (2021). *The Meaning of Work in the 21st Century.* Oxford University Press.

Chapter 18: The 50 Most Wanted Jobs of the Future

Introduction

In this chapter, we explore the 50 jobs that I expect will be most in demand over the coming decades. These predictions are based on current technological advancements, societal shifts, environmental challenges, and evolving economic needs. While these jobs reflect my vision of the future, they are also grounded in existing trends and research about the impact of artificial intelligence, automation, sustainability, and globalization on the workforce.

As industries continue to be disrupted by technology, entirely new categories of jobs are emerging, many of which did not exist just a few years ago. Fields like artificial intelligence, biotechnology, and green energy are at the forefront of this change, while traditional roles are being redefined through digital transformation. This chapter will provide an overview of the top 50 jobs expected to dominate the future landscape, along with a brief description of each role. By the end of this chapter, readers will have a clear understanding of where future job opportunities are likely to arise and what skills will be in demand.

Note: These predictions are based on logical forecasts of how current trends may evolve and should be seen as one possible future. The future is inherently uncertain, but by staying informed and prepared, individuals can position themselves to take advantage of emerging opportunities.

Expanded List of Jobs with References and Logic

1. **AI Specialist**

   As artificial intelligence (AI) continues to transform industries, demand for AI specialists will surge. These professionals develop AI systems, which are used in automation, personalized services, and advanced decision-making. According to McKinsey's report on AI adoption, businesses that embrace AI will see significant productivity gains in areas such as customer service, healthcare diagnostics, and financial analysis . AI specialists require a background in machine learning, deep learning, and natural language processing.

2. **Machine Learning Engineer**

   With machine learning (ML) being the backbone of AI advancements, ML engineers will become highly sought-after for building algorithms that enable machines to learn from data and improve over time. These roles are especially important for fields like autonomous vehicles, predictive analytics, and healthcare diagnostics . Companies like Tesla and Google rely heavily on ML engineers to push the boundaries of AI technology.

3. **Data Scientist**

   Data is considered the "new oil," and data scientists will be at the forefront of turning vast amounts of information into actionable insights. As companies rely more on big data for decision-making, professionals who can analyze and interpret data will be essential in industries ranging from finance to retail. A data scientist needs a strong foundation in statistics, programming, and data visualization.

4. **Cybersecurity Analyst**

   As cyber threats continue to rise, cybersecurity has become a top priority for governments and businesses alike. The growing reliance on cloud computing, remote work, and digital infrastructures makes organizations vulnerable to attacks. Cybersecurity analysts will be tasked with protecting networks and sensitive data from breaches. This role requires proficiency in encryption, ethical hacking, and security protocols.

5. **Robotics Engineer**

   Robotics is transforming industries like manufacturing, healthcare, and agriculture by automating repetitive tasks and improving efficiency. As companies adopt robots to streamline production, reduce errors, and enhance precision, robotics engineers will play a critical role. With the rise of collaborative robots (cobots) that work alongside humans, this field will grow significantly. Skills needed include mechanical engineering, computer programming, and robotics system design.

6. **Quantum Computing Scientist**

    Quantum computing is expected to revolutionize fields that require complex problem-solving, such as pharmaceuticals, cryptography, and logistics. Quantum computers, which process data in qubits instead of traditional bits, can solve problems that are currently beyond the reach of classical computers. As quantum technology matures, quantum computing scientists will be in high demand to unlock its potential. This requires expertise in quantum mechanics, mathematics, and computer science.

7. **Biotechnology Engineer**

    Biotechnology engineers apply biological systems to develop innovative technologies, particularly in healthcare and agriculture. Advances in genetic engineering, such as CRISPR, and bio-manufacturing are creating new opportunities in personalized medicine, sustainable agriculture, and even environmental cleanup. Professionals in this field need knowledge of biology, chemistry, and engineering, and they will be crucial in solving some of humanity's biggest challenges, from disease to food security.

8. **Genetic Counselor**

   As personalized medicine grows, more individuals will seek genetic counseling to understand their genetic profiles and the risks associated with inherited diseases. This role will become especially relevant as genetic testing becomes more accessible . Genetic counselors need strong communication skills to explain complex genetic information to patients and a solid understanding of genetics and healthcare.

9. **Renewable Energy Technician**

   As the world shifts toward renewable energy to combat climate change, technicians who can install and maintain renewable energy systems, such as solar, wind, and hydropower, will be vital. According to the International Renewable Energy Agency (IRENA), the renewable energy sector is expected to create over 40 million jobs by 2050 . These technicians require skills in electrical systems, mechanical engineering, and renewable technologies.

10. **Sustainability Specialist**

    Sustainability specialists help businesses and governments adopt environmentally friendly practices to reduce their carbon footprints and improve resource efficiency. With growing pressure from consumers and regulations to address climate change, sustainability experts will play a key role in shaping future business strategies . This job requires knowledge of environmental science, corporate responsibility, and government policies.

11. **Telemedicine Specialist**

The healthcare industry is rapidly adopting telemedicine, a trend accelerated by the COVID-19 pandemic. Telemedicine specialists facilitate remote patient care through digital platforms, which not only increases access to healthcare but also reduces costs. The rise of wearable health devices and AI-assisted diagnostics will further drive the need for telemedicine professionals . Specialists must be skilled in healthcare protocols, patient communication, and health tech tools like video conferencing and digital records management.

12. **VR/AR Developer**

Virtual reality (VR) and augmented reality (AR) are increasingly being used in industries such as gaming, education, and training. As VR/AR technologies advance, developers will be needed to create immersive environments for entertainment, simulations, and even therapeutic uses in healthcare . With companies like Facebook (Meta) investing heavily in the metaverse, VR/AR developers will be critical in shaping the future of digital interaction. Skills include 3D modeling, programming, and virtual environment design.

13. **Space Engineer**

    Space exploration is entering a new phase of commercialization, led by companies like SpaceX, Blue Origin, and traditional space agencies. Space engineers design, build, and maintain spacecraft, satellites, and related technologies. With plans for moon bases, Mars missions, and space tourism, this field will expand significantly . Aerospace engineering, physics, and robotics are essential skills for this role.

14. **AI Ethicist**

    As AI systems take on more significant roles in decision-making, concerns about bias, privacy, and accountability have emerged. AI ethicists will ensure that AI systems are designed and deployed in ways that are ethical and socially responsible . This role will become increasingly important as AI applications permeate areas like criminal justice, healthcare, and hiring. AI ethicists need a background in philosophy, ethics, and AI technology.

15. **Autonomous Vehicle Engineer**

    Self-driving cars and autonomous vehicles (AVs) are set to disrupt transportation. As companies like Tesla and Waymo push forward with AV technology, engineers who can develop and maintain these systems will be in high demand . This job involves building the sensors, algorithms, and software that enable vehicles to navigate and make decisions without human input. Expertise in machine learning, robotics, and automotive engineering is required.

16. **Blockchain Developer**

    Blockchain technology, best known for its role in cryptocurrencies like Bitcoin, is finding applications in industries ranging from supply chain management to secure voting systems. Blockchain developers create decentralized applications that enhance security and transparency . With businesses exploring blockchain for contract management, digital identity, and secure transactions, demand for developers with knowledge of cryptography and blockchain frameworks will grow.

17. **3D Printing Technician**

    3D printing is revolutionizing manufacturing by enabling rapid prototyping and the production of complex parts with minimal waste. Industries like healthcare, automotive, and aerospace are adopting 3D printing to create customized products on-demand . 3D printing technicians need expertise in materials science, CAD software, and machine maintenance to operate these additive manufacturing systems.

18. **Climate Change Analyst**

    Climate change analysts study environmental data to assess the effects of global warming and help organizations mitigate their environmental impact. With climate change accelerating, governments and businesses are investing in strategies to reduce carbon emissions and adapt to environmental challenges . Analysts in this field need a background in environmental science, data analysis, and policy-making.

19. **Healthcare Data Analyst**

    Healthcare is increasingly data-driven, with hospitals and providers using data to improve patient care, optimize operations, and track public health trends. Healthcare data analysts help organizations make sense of complex datasets, from electronic health records to population health statistics . Skills in data analysis tools, such as SQL and Python, and a strong understanding of healthcare systems are required.

20. **Food Scientist**

    Global food production faces challenges from climate change, resource scarcity, and population growth. Food scientists will play a critical role in developing sustainable food solutions, including lab-grown meat, plant-based proteins, and biofortified crops . Expertise in biochemistry, nutrition, and food safety will be essential as the world seeks to address food security through innovation.

21. **Green Building Architect**

    The future of architecture lies in sustainability, with green building architects designing energy-efficient structures that minimize environmental impact. As urbanization increases, architects who specialize in eco-friendly designs, using renewable materials and smart technologies, will be in high demand . This job requires knowledge of architecture, environmental science, and sustainable construction techniques.

22. **Digital Twin Specialist**

Digital twin technology creates virtual models of physical systems, such as buildings or industrial equipment, to monitor performance and predict maintenance needs. Industries like manufacturing, real estate, and urban planning are adopting digital twins to optimize operations . Specialists need expertise in IoT, simulation software, and data analytics to create and manage these virtual models.

23. **Personalized Healthcare Advisor**

Personalized healthcare tailors treatment plans to individual patients based on genetic, lifestyle, and environmental data. As genetic testing becomes more affordable, healthcare providers will need personalized healthcare advisors to interpret this data and develop customized treatment strategies . A strong background in genetics, healthcare, and patient communication is essential.

24. **Smart City Planner**

With global urbanization on the rise, cities are adopting smart technologies to improve quality of life, sustainability, and efficiency. Smart city planners design urban environments that integrate renewable energy, IoT systems, and efficient transportation networks . This role will be crucial as cities adapt to population growth and environmental pressures. Key skills include urban planning, civil engineering, and technology integration.

25. **Cloud Engineer**

As more businesses move their operations to the cloud, cloud engineers will be needed to design, build, and manage cloud infrastructure. Cloud computing allows companies to scale operations quickly and securely, making cloud engineers indispensable for organizations embracing digital transformation . Expertise in cloud platforms like AWS, Azure, and Google Cloud is critical for this role.

26. **AI-Powered Marketing Specialist**

AI-driven marketing is revolutionizing how businesses engage with customers, offering personalized and data-driven insights. AI-powered marketing specialists will leverage AI tools to optimize ad targeting, customer segmentation, and engagement strategies . Skills in AI, digital marketing, and data analysis will be essential for this role.

27. **Drone Operator/Engineer**

    Drones are being used for everything from package delivery to agricultural monitoring and infrastructure inspection. As the commercial use of drones expands, operators and engineers will be needed to manage drone fleets, ensure regulatory compliance, and design new drone applications. This role requires expertise in robotics, aviation regulations, and drone technology.

28. **Tech Wearable Designer**

    Wearable technologies, such as smartwatches and fitness trackers, are increasingly integrated into daily life. Designers of wearable tech focus on creating devices that enhance health, productivity, and connectivity. The demand for new wearable technologies will continue to grow, requiring skills in hardware design, user experience (UX), and sensor integration.

29. **Agricultural Technologist**

    The future of agriculture depends on technology to improve yields, reduce waste, and adapt to changing environmental conditions. Agricultural technologists will develop and implement advanced farming technologies such as precision farming, drone monitoring, and AI-powered crop management. A background in agricultural science, engineering, and data analysis will be essential.

30. **AI-Driven Content Creator**

    AI-generated content is transforming industries like entertainment, media, and marketing. AI-driven content creators will use AI tools to generate high-quality content at scale, whether it's articles, videos, or social media posts . This role will require a blend of creative skills, digital marketing knowledge, and familiarity with AI content-generation tools like GPT and DALL·E.

Let's continue with the next set of expanded job descriptions, including references and logical support for why these roles will be essential in the future.

31. **Digital Currency Advisor**

    As the use of cryptocurrencies and decentralized finance (DeFi) expands, digital currency advisors will help individuals and businesses navigate this new financial landscape. These professionals will provide expertise on digital assets, blockchain technology, and regulatory compliance . With the rise of digital currencies like Bitcoin and Ethereum, digital currency advisors need a solid foundation in finance, blockchain, and fintech.

32. **Mental Health Tech Specialist**

    Technology is playing a growing role in mental health treatment, from teletherapy to AI-powered mental health apps. Mental health tech specialists will design and implement technologies that improve access to mental health care and enhance treatment outcomes . This role requires a deep understanding of both mental health issues and the technology used in therapeutic interventions.

33. **Elder Care Tech Consultant**

    With an aging global population, elder care is becoming a critical issue. Elder care tech consultants will help develop and implement technologies that allow older adults to live independently for longer, such as health monitoring devices, AI-powered home assistants, and telemedicine platforms . Consultants in this field need expertise in gerontology, health tech, and elder care services.

34. **AI-Powered Customer Service Agent**

    AI is revolutionizing customer service by automating routine inquiries and offering personalized solutions. AI-powered customer service agents use machine learning and natural language processing to improve response times and customer satisfaction . As more companies adopt AI-driven support systems, individuals skilled in deploying and maintaining these technologies will be in demand.

35. **Smart Home Technician**

    Smart home technologies are becoming more widespread, allowing homeowners to control lighting, security, appliances, and climate systems remotely. Smart home technicians install and maintain these systems, ensuring they work seamlessly and securely . This job requires expertise in IoT (Internet of Things), networking, and home automation systems.

36. **Waste Management Engineer**

    As the world grapples with waste disposal challenges, waste management engineers will play a crucial role in developing sustainable waste solutions. They design systems for waste reduction, recycling, and converting waste into energy . This job is vital as cities and industries look for innovative ways to handle growing amounts of waste. Environmental engineering, chemistry, and waste processing technology are key skills.

37. **Food Delivery Logistics Manager**

    With the rise of online food delivery services and automated logistics systems, food delivery logistics managers will be needed to oversee supply chains, optimize delivery routes, and manage food safety standards . This role combines traditional logistics management with new technologies like AI-driven route optimization and drone delivery systems.

38. **Ethical Hacker (Penetration Tester)**

    Ethical hackers, also known as penetration testers, simulate cyberattacks to identify and fix vulnerabilities in an organization's security systems. As cyber threats grow in frequency and complexity, ethical hackers will be increasingly important in protecting sensitive data and critical infrastructure . Skills in network security, coding, and cryptography are crucial for this role.

39. **Quantum Data Analyst**

    Quantum computing promises to solve problems that are impossible for classical computers, particularly in data-heavy fields like cryptography, finance, and scientific research. Quantum data analysts will work with quantum computers to process and analyze vast datasets, unlocking new insights . A deep understanding of quantum mechanics, mathematics, and data science is required for this emerging field.

40. **Circular Economy Consultant**

    Circular economy consultants help businesses transition from traditional linear models of production to circular models, where products are designed for reuse, recycling, or regeneration. This shift is critical as companies look for ways to reduce waste and meet sustainability goals . Knowledge of sustainability, supply chain management, and green technologies is essential for this role.

41. **VR Therapy Specialist**

    Virtual reality is being used in therapy to treat conditions such as PTSD, anxiety, and chronic pain by immersing patients in controlled virtual environments. VR therapy specialists design and administer these programs, providing a new avenue for mental health treatment . This role requires expertise in psychology, VR technology, and patient care.

42. **E-Sports Coach**

E-sports, or competitive video gaming, has grown into a billion-dollar industry with millions of fans worldwide. E-sports coaches train professional gamers and teams, helping them improve their skills, strategies, and teamwork . With the continued rise of e-sports leagues and tournaments, demand for coaches with deep knowledge of gaming strategies and sports psychology will grow.

43. **AI Legal Consultant**

As AI systems become more integrated into business and society, legal questions regarding data privacy, intellectual property, liability, and ethical use will arise. AI legal consultants will provide advice on navigating the complex legal landscape surrounding AI technologies . Professionals in this role will need a background in law, ethics, and AI technologies.

44. **Electric Vehicle Technician**

As the automotive industry transitions to electric vehicles (EVs), technicians who can repair and maintain EVs will be in high demand. This role involves working with specialized electric drivetrains, batteries, and charging systems . With governments around the world pushing for greener transportation, EV technicians will be critical to supporting this transition.

45. **AI-Powered Financial Advisor**

    Financial advisors who leverage AI to analyze market trends, assess risk, and provide personalized investment advice will be highly sought after. AI-powered financial advisors will use machine learning algorithms to make faster and more accurate financial predictions, improving client outcomes . This job requires a combination of finance expertise and knowledge of AI tools.

46. **Telework Coordinator**

    As remote work becomes more common, telework coordinators will help organizations manage decentralized workforces by optimizing productivity, communication, and digital collaboration. This role is vital as companies adopt hybrid work models that combine in-office and remote work . Knowledge of remote work technologies, project management, and HR practices is essential for this job.

47. **VR Travel Experience Designer**

    Virtual reality is transforming how people experience travel, with VR travel experience designers creating immersive virtual tours of destinations. These professionals use VR to offer travel experiences that replicate real-world environments, allowing people to explore new places from the comfort of their homes . Skills in VR development, storytelling, and tourism are needed for this role.

48. **Social Media Influencer Manager**

    As influencer marketing grows in popularity, social media influencer managers will help brands connect with online personalities to promote products and services. These managers will oversee partnerships, ensure brand alignment, and track campaign performance . Expertise in social media trends, marketing strategies, and influencer relations is crucial.

49. **Crisis Management Specialist**

    Crisis management specialists help organizations prepare for and respond to emergencies, such as natural disasters, cyberattacks, or public relations crises. They develop risk mitigation strategies and coordinate responses to minimize damage . This role requires expertise in risk management, communication, and emergency response planning.

50. **Smart Grid Engineer**

    Smart grid engineers design and maintain electrical grids that integrate renewable energy sources, energy storage, and digital control systems. As the energy sector shifts towards more sustainable power sources, smart grids will be essential for managing energy distribution efficiently and reliably . Electrical engineering, renewable energy, and IoT are key skills for this job.

References

- McKinsey & Company. (2021). *The State of AI Adoption*. Retrieved from [mckinsey.com].
- International Renewable Energy Agency (IRENA). (2019). *Future of Renewable Energy*. Retrieved from [irena.org].
- World Economic Forum. (2020). *The Future of Jobs Report*. Retrieved from [weforum.org].

Chapter 19: AI Specialist

Job Definition

An AI Specialist is responsible for developing, implementing, and maintaining artificial intelligence systems that enable machines to perform tasks typically requiring human intelligence. This can include anything from chatbots and virtual assistants to complex AI systems used in industries like healthcare, finance, and retail. AI Specialists use machine learning, deep learning, and natural language processing to create intelligent systems that can automate tasks, make decisions, and improve over time.

How to Prepare for the Job

To become an AI Specialist, individuals should focus on acquiring skills in computer science, mathematics, and data science. A bachelor's degree in one of these fields is usually required, with many professionals pursuing a master's or PhD in AI or machine learning. Learning to program in languages such as Python, Java, and C++ is essential, as is becoming familiar with machine learning frameworks like TensorFlow, Keras, and PyTorch.

Other ways to prepare include:

- **Online courses**: Many platforms like Coursera and Udacity offer AI and machine learning courses taught by industry experts.
- **Certifications**: Getting certified in AI or machine learning (e.g., Google AI Certification, IBM AI Engineering Professional Certificate) can boost your credentials.
- **Projects and Competitions**: Participate in AI competitions on platforms like Kaggle to build a portfolio of AI projects and gain hands-on experience.

Basic Information and Structure of Learning

- **Programming skills**: Python is widely used in AI development, so proficiency in Python and libraries such as NumPy, Pandas, and Scikit-learn is critical.
- **Mathematics and statistics**: AI specialists need a solid foundation in linear algebra, probability, and statistics.
- **Data science**: Understanding how to work with large datasets is important for training AI systems.
- **AI frameworks**: Experience with frameworks like TensorFlow, Keras, and PyTorch is essential for building machine learning models.

- **Ethics and AI**: Learning about the ethical implications of AI, such as data privacy and bias, is becoming increasingly important.

Important Insights about the Job

The future of AI is rapidly evolving, with applications across numerous industries. AI Specialists will find opportunities in sectors such as healthcare (for diagnostics and drug discovery), finance (for fraud detection and algorithmic trading), and retail (for customer personalization and supply chain optimization). The demand for AI expertise is expected to grow significantly, with AI transforming business models and creating efficiency in decision-making processes.

Tips and Advice (Dos and Don'ts)

Dos:

- **Stay updated**: AI is a fast-evolving field, so staying current with the latest advancements is essential. Follow AI blogs, attend conferences, and take part in professional networks.
- **Build a strong portfolio**: Showcase your AI projects on platforms like GitHub or Kaggle to demonstrate your expertise to potential employers.

- **Understand ethics**: As AI systems increasingly impact society, understanding ethical issues such as bias and fairness in AI is critical.

Don'ts:

- **Don't focus only on theory**: Practical experience is just as important as theoretical knowledge in AI. Focus on building real-world projects.
- **Don't ignore the math**: AI relies heavily on mathematical concepts, so be sure not to neglect this foundational aspect.

Resources and Links for Further Learning

- **Coursera AI Courses**: AI Specializations on Coursera
- **Deep Learning Specialization by Andrew Ng**: Coursera
- **Kaggle**: A platform for AI competitions and datasets: www.kaggle.com
- **Books**: *Artificial Intelligence: A Modern Approach* by Stuart Russell and Peter Norvig

Chapter 20: Cybersecurity Analyst

Job Definition

Cybersecurity analysts are responsible for protecting an organization's digital infrastructure from cyberattacks, data breaches, and other security threats. They monitor networks for vulnerabilities, develop security protocols, and respond to security incidents. As businesses continue to digitize their operations, cybersecurity analysts will become increasingly important to safeguard sensitive data and prevent costly attacks.

How to Prepare for the Job

To become a cybersecurity analyst, individuals typically need a degree in computer science, information technology, or cybersecurity. In addition to formal education, practical experience in network security and hands-on knowledge of security tools is crucial.

Steps to prepare include:

- **Learning network security fundamentals**: Familiarize yourself with firewalls, VPNs, encryption, and intrusion detection systems (IDS).
- **Obtaining certifications**: Industry-recognized certifications like Certified Information Systems Security Professional

(CISSP), CompTIA Security+, and Certified Ethical Hacker (CEH) are essential for career advancement.
- **Gaining hands-on experience**: Set up your own home lab to practice identifying and mitigating security vulnerabilities.

Basic Information and Structure of Learning

- **Network security**: Learn how to protect data as it moves through networks using firewalls, VPNs, and other security measures.
- **Ethical hacking**: Ethical hackers use penetration testing to find vulnerabilities in systems before malicious actors can exploit them.
- **Risk management**: Understanding how to assess risks and develop strategies to mitigate them is key in this role.
- **Security tools**: Knowledge of security tools like Wireshark, Metasploit, and Nessus is essential for detecting and analyzing threats.

Important Insights about the Job

With the rise of remote work, cloud computing, and IoT, the attack surface for cybercriminals has expanded. Cybersecurity analysts will play a pivotal role in protecting data and systems from increasingly sophisticated cyberattacks. This role is critical in industries like finance, healthcare, and government, where data breaches can have severe consequences. As cybersecurity becomes more embedded in business operations, cybersecurity professionals with a broad skill set will be in high demand.

Tips and Advice (Dos and Don'ts)

Dos:

- **Keep learning**: Cybersecurity threats evolve constantly, so continuous learning is necessary to stay ahead of attackers.
- **Gain real-world experience**: Participate in Capture The Flag (CTF) events or take part in security internships to build practical skills.
- **Be ethical**: Always follow legal and ethical guidelines in your work, especially when performing penetration testing.

Don'ts:

- **Don't rely solely on tools**: While security tools are important, understanding the underlying principles of cybersecurity is crucial.
- **Don't underestimate human error**: Many cyber incidents are caused by human mistakes, so cybersecurity analysts should focus on training employees in security best practices.

Resources and Links for Further Learning

- **Cybrary**: Free and paid cybersecurity training: www.cybrary.it
- **CompTIA Security+ Certification**: CompTIA
- **SANS Institute**: Professional cybersecurity training: www.sans.org
- **Books**: *The Web Application Hacker's Handbook* by Dafydd Stuttard and Marcus Pinto

Chapter 21: Biotechnology Engineer

Job Definition

Biotechnology engineers apply biological and engineering principles to develop technologies that improve healthcare, agriculture, and environmental sustainability. Their work includes genetic engineering, bio-manufacturing, and developing medical devices. As personalized medicine and sustainable agriculture gain prominence, biotechnology engineers will play a critical role in addressing global challenges such as food security and healthcare innovation.

How to Prepare for the Job

To become a biotechnology engineer, individuals typically need a degree in biomedical engineering, biotechnology, or a related field like molecular biology. Advanced degrees (master's or PhD) are often required for specialized roles in genetic engineering or pharmaceuticals. Experience in laboratory work, bioinformatics, and a deep understanding of biology and chemistry are essential for success in this field.

Steps to prepare include:

- **Earn a degree in biotechnology**: Undergraduate degrees in biotech, bioengineering, or molecular biology provide foundational knowledge.
- **Pursue internships or lab work**: Hands-on experience in research labs or biotech companies will be invaluable.
- **Specialize through advanced courses**: Focus on areas such as genetic engineering, CRISPR technology, or bio-manufacturing processes through master's programs or certifications.

Basic Information and Structure of Learning

- **Biological sciences**: A strong understanding of molecular biology, genetics, and cell biology is crucial for designing biotech solutions.
- **Engineering principles**: Biotechnology engineers must also apply engineering concepts, such as systems design, fluid mechanics, and thermodynamics, to biological processes.
- **Lab work**: Mastering techniques like gene editing, PCR (polymerase chain reaction), and bioreactor management is essential.
- **Bioinformatics**: The ability to analyze biological data using software tools is increasingly important in biotechnology.

Important Insights about the Job

Biotechnology engineers are at the intersection of biology and technology, developing innovations that impact everything from healthcare to environmental sustainability. As the demand for sustainable food sources and advanced medical treatments grows, biotech engineers will be instrumental in creating solutions. The field is driven by advances in areas like gene editing (CRISPR), personalized medicine, and synthetic biology, making it one of the most exciting fields for the future.

Tips and Advice (Dos and Don'ts)

Dos:

- **Stay curious**: Biotechnology is constantly evolving, so staying up to date with the latest research is vital.
- **Get hands-on experience**: Laboratory skills and real-world applications of biotech processes are crucial for building expertise.
- **Pursue interdisciplinary knowledge**: Biotech engineers need to understand both biological and engineering principles, so develop a broad skill set.

Don'ts:

- **Don't neglect bioethics**: Understanding the ethical implications of biotechnology, especially in areas like genetic engineering, is critical.
- **Don't overlook regulations**: Biotechnology is heavily regulated, so engineers need to be familiar with industry standards and compliance requirements.

Resources and Links for Further Learning

- **MIT OpenCourseWare**: Biotechnology and bioengineering courses: MIT OCW
- **Biotechnology Certification Programs**: Various certification options for specialized biotech fields: Coursera Biotechnology Courses
- **Books**: *Biotechnology: A Laboratory Skills Course* by Jennifer Reczek and *Molecular Biotechnology* by Bernard Glick

Chapter 22: Renewable Energy Technician

Job Definition

Renewable energy technicians are responsible for installing, maintaining, and repairing systems that harness power from renewable sources, such as solar, wind, and hydropower. These professionals are essential as the world transitions to more sustainable energy systems to combat climate change. Technicians ensure that renewable energy systems operate efficiently and safely, playing a key role in the expansion of green energy.

How to Prepare for the Job

To become a renewable energy technician, individuals can pursue vocational training or associate degrees in renewable energy technology. Specialized training programs focused on solar or wind energy are also available. Hands-on experience with electrical systems, mechanical repairs, and energy storage systems is crucial for success in this field.

Steps to prepare include:

- **Enroll in a renewable energy program**: Technical schools and community colleges offer programs in solar, wind, and energy management systems.
- **Gain hands-on experience**: Apprenticeships or internships with renewable energy companies provide practical experience.
- **Get certified**: Certifications such as the North American Board of Certified Energy Practitioners (NABCEP) Solar PV Installer Certification can enhance your employability.

Basic Information and Structure of Learning

- **Electrical and mechanical systems**: Technicians must understand how renewable energy systems, such as solar panels and wind turbines, generate and store power.
- **Energy storage**: Knowledge of battery systems and energy storage technologies is critical as renewable energy often needs to be stored for later use.
- **Safety protocols**: Renewable energy technicians must adhere to safety standards when working with electrical systems and heights (e.g., wind turbines).
- **Maintenance**: Technicians regularly inspect systems for wear and perform repairs to ensure optimal performance.

Important Insights about the Job

The shift towards renewable energy is one of the most significant trends of the 21st century, with governments and businesses investing heavily in green energy projects. According to the International Renewable Energy Agency (IRENA), the renewable energy sector could create 40 million jobs by 2050. Renewable energy technicians are essential in ensuring that solar, wind, and other renewable power systems function efficiently, helping reduce the world's reliance on fossil fuels.

Tips and Advice (Dos and Don'ts)

Dos:

- **Get hands-on experience**: The renewable energy field requires practical knowledge of systems installation and maintenance, so focus on gaining field experience.
- **Stay updated on new technologies**: Renewable energy technologies evolve rapidly, so staying informed about the latest advancements in energy storage and grid integration is essential.

- **Prioritize safety**: Renewable energy work, especially on wind turbines and electrical systems, can be hazardous, so following safety protocols is critical.

Don'ts:

- **Don't underestimate certifications**: Industry-recognized certifications can make you more competitive in the job market.
- **Don't ignore environmental regulations**: Understanding local and international regulations regarding renewable energy installations is important for compliance.

Resources and Links for Further Learning

- **IREC Training**: Renewable energy training resources: IREC
- **NABCEP Certification**: Solar PV Installer Certification: NABCEP
- **Books**: *Renewable Energy: Power for a Sustainable Future* by Godfrey Boyle and *The Renewable Energy Handbook* by William Kemp

Chapter 23: Quantum Computing Scientist

Job Definition

Quantum computing scientists work on the development of quantum computers, which use quantum bits (qubits) to perform calculations far beyond the capabilities of classical computers. These scientists are at the forefront of solving complex problems in fields such as cryptography, chemistry, and finance. Quantum computing is expected to revolutionize industries by providing breakthroughs in areas that require vast computational power.

How to Prepare for the Job

Becoming a quantum computing scientist requires a strong foundation in mathematics, computer science, and quantum mechanics. Most professionals in this field have advanced degrees (master's or PhD) in quantum physics, computer science, or a related field. Specializing in quantum algorithms, quantum hardware, or quantum cryptography can open opportunities in academia, industry, or research labs.

Steps to prepare include:

- **Pursue advanced education**: A PhD in quantum physics, computer science, or electrical engineering is often required.
- **Learn quantum programming languages**: Become proficient in quantum programming environments like Qiskit, Cirq, and Microsoft's Quantum Development Kit.
- **Focus on quantum mechanics**: Mastering the principles of quantum mechanics is essential to understanding how quantum computing works.

Basic Information and Structure of Learning

- **Quantum physics**: Understanding the principles of quantum mechanics, such as superposition and entanglement, is fundamental to quantum computing.
- **Quantum algorithms**: Scientists must develop algorithms that take advantage of quantum parallelism to solve complex problems faster than classical computers.
- **Quantum hardware**: Knowledge of quantum hardware, such as quantum gates and quantum circuits, is necessary for building functional quantum computers.
- **Quantum cryptography**: As quantum computers can potentially break classical encryption methods, quantum cryptography is a growing field for secure communications.

Important Insights about the Job

Quantum computing is still in its early stages but holds immense potential for transforming industries such as cryptography, pharmaceuticals, and finance. Quantum computers can solve problems that are currently intractable for classical computers, such as simulating complex molecular structures or optimizing supply chains. Companies like IBM, Google, and Microsoft are investing heavily in quantum research, making this field one of the most exciting frontiers in computing.

Tips and Advice (Dos and Don'ts)

Dos:

- **Pursue advanced research**: Quantum computing is an emerging field, so staying involved in cutting-edge research and publications is crucial.
- **Build expertise in both theory and practice**: Quantum computing scientists need a deep understanding of theoretical quantum physics as well as practical skills in quantum programming.

- **Collaborate**: The interdisciplinary nature of quantum computing means that collaboration with physicists, engineers, and computer scientists is essential for success.

Don'ts:

- **Don't ignore classical computing**: While quantum computing is the focus, an understanding of classical computing principles is still necessary for integrating quantum systems.
- **Don't expect immediate commercialization**: Quantum computing is still in the experimental phase, so manage expectations regarding practical applications in the near future.

Resources and Links for Further Learning

- **IBM Qiskit**: Open-source quantum computing software: Qiskit
- **Quantum Computing for the Very Curious**: A free book on quantum computing fundamentals: Quantum Country
- **Books**: *Quantum Computing: A Gentle Introduction* by Eleanor Rieffel and Wolfgang Polak and *Quantum Computation and Quantum Information* by Michael Nielsen and Isaac Chuang

Chapter 24: Preparing for Future Jobs – Practical Tips and Advice

General Tips for Future-Proofing Your Career

In this chapter, we will provide general advice that applies across all industries and jobs. With the rapid pace of change in the job market, individuals need to focus on adaptability, continuous learning, and developing the right mindset to stay competitive.

1. Lifelong Learning and Upskilling

As the future job market continues to evolve, one thing is clear: continuous learning is no longer optional; it's essential. Many of the most in-demand jobs require skills that didn't exist a few years ago, and that trend will only accelerate. Whether you're an AI specialist, a healthcare worker, or a renewable energy technician, committing to lifelong learning will be your greatest asset.

Tips for Lifelong Learning:

- **Enroll in Online Courses**: Platforms like Coursera, edX, and Udemy offer courses on everything from AI to leadership skills. You can earn certifications from top universities and industry experts.

- **Attend Webinars and Conferences**: Stay updated with industry trends by attending virtual conferences, webinars, or workshops in your field.
- **Read Industry Blogs and Research Papers**: Following leading thinkers and researchers in your field will help you stay on top of new trends and technologies.
- **Learn on the Job**: Embrace learning opportunities within your current role by taking on new projects that push your boundaries or by cross-training with colleagues in different departments.

2. Develop Digital and Data Literacy

No matter the industry, digital literacy is becoming a non-negotiable skill. As technology continues to integrate into everyday business operations, individuals who are comfortable working with digital tools and analyzing data will have a significant advantage.

Key Skills to Focus On:

- **Basic Programming**: Learning to code, even at a basic level, can open doors to automation and more efficient work processes. Python is a great starting point.
- **Data Analysis**: Every industry is data-driven. Familiarize yourself with data analysis tools like Excel, SQL, or Python's data science libraries (Pandas, NumPy).

- **Cloud Computing**: Understanding how cloud systems work and how they are used in businesses (AWS, Google Cloud, Azure) will be critical as more companies migrate to the cloud.
- **Digital Collaboration Tools**: Tools like Slack, Microsoft Teams, and Zoom are essential for remote work and digital collaboration, which are becoming more common in almost every field.

3. Cultivate Adaptability and Resilience

The ability to adapt to new situations and pivot when necessary will be one of the most valuable traits in the future job market. With technologies like AI, automation, and robotics reshaping industries, individuals will need to embrace change rather than resist it.

Practical Steps to Build Adaptability:

- **Stay Open to New Opportunities**: Be willing to switch roles, try new industries, or take on projects outside your comfort zone. Flexibility is key in a fast-changing job market.
- **Develop a Growth Mindset**: Embrace challenges and see failures as opportunities to learn. According to psychologist Carol Dweck's research, individuals with a growth mindset are more likely to succeed in uncertain environments.

- **Practice Problem-Solving**: Sharpen your problem-solving skills by tackling complex projects or engaging in exercises like design thinking and case studies.

4. Build Interdisciplinary Knowledge

The future of work will increasingly blur the lines between disciplines. For example, AI specialists will need a good understanding of ethics and law, while healthcare workers may need to learn about data science and AI for diagnostics. Cultivating interdisciplinary skills will make you more valuable in an interconnected world.

How to Build Interdisciplinary Skills:

- **Explore Adjacent Fields**: If you're a data scientist, learn about business strategy; if you're in healthcare, explore AI-driven diagnostics. Expanding your skill set will make you more versatile.
- **Collaborate with Diverse Teams**: Working with professionals from different fields exposes you to new ways of thinking and problem-solving.
- **Read Widely**: Don't limit your learning to your specific industry. Reading about different industries can give you a fresh perspective on problem-solving and innovation.

5. Master Communication and Soft Skills

While technical skills are crucial, soft skills like communication, leadership, and teamwork will remain equally important in the future job market. As workplaces become more digital and remote, the ability to clearly articulate ideas, collaborate across teams, and lead effectively will set you apart.

Essential Soft Skills:

- **Emotional Intelligence (EQ)**: EQ is the ability to understand and manage your emotions and those of others. It's critical for teamwork, leadership, and customer relations.
- **Collaboration**: Learn how to work effectively in remote and hybrid teams using digital communication tools.
- **Leadership**: Whether or not you're in a managerial role, leadership skills are important. You can lead by taking initiative, mentoring others, or spearheading new projects.
- **Problem-Solving and Creativity**: As automation handles routine tasks, creativity and problem-solving will become differentiating skills in many industries.

6. Stay Ahead of Technological Trends

Technological advancements are happening at an unprecedented rate, and staying informed about these trends is crucial for preparing for future jobs. Being proactive in learning about new technologies will allow you to position yourself at the forefront of innovation.

Technologies to Watch:

- **Artificial Intelligence and Machine Learning**: AI is impacting every sector, from healthcare to marketing. Understanding how it works and how it can be applied in your industry is critical.
- **Blockchain Technology**: Blockchain isn't just for cryptocurrencies; it's also transforming industries like supply chain management, voting systems, and intellectual property protection.
- **Quantum Computing**: Although still in its early stages, quantum computing is set to revolutionize industries that require complex problem-solving capabilities.
- **5G and IoT**: As 5G networks expand, the Internet of Things (IoT) will connect everything from smart homes to autonomous vehicles. Understanding these technologies will be important for future roles.

Chapter 25: Preparing for Specific Future Jobs (Based on the Top 50)

This chapter will provide tailored tips and resources for readers interested in preparing for the jobs listed in **Chapter 1: The 50 Most Wanted Jobs**.

1. AI Specialist

Key Skills to Focus On:

- Machine Learning
- Python and TensorFlow
- Data Analysis and Big Data
- AI Ethics

Useful Resources:

- **Coursera's AI Specialization**
- **Google AI Certification**
- **Kaggle Competitions for Hands-on Experience**

2. Cybersecurity Analyst

Key Skills to Focus On:

- Network Security

- Ethical Hacking
- Risk Management
- Security Tools like Wireshark and Metasploit

Useful Resources:

- CompTIA Security+ Certification
- Certified Ethical Hacker (CEH) Training
- Cybrary Security Courses

3. Biotechnology Engineer

Key Skills to Focus On:

- Genetic Engineering (CRISPR)
- Bioinformatics
- Molecular Biology
- Laboratory Techniques

Useful Resources:

- MIT OpenCourseWare in Biotechnology
- Online Lab Courses and Certifications in Biotech

4. Renewable Energy Technician

Key Skills to Focus On:

- Electrical and Mechanical Systems
- Solar and Wind Energy Systems
- Energy Storage Technologies
- Maintenance and Safety Protocols

Useful Resources:

- IREC's Renewable Energy Training Programs
- NABCEP Solar PV Installer Certification

5. Quantum Computing Scientist

Key Skills to Focus On:

- Quantum Physics and Algorithms
- Quantum Programming Languages (Qiskit, Cirq)
- Quantum Cryptography

Useful Resources:

- IBM Qiskit Tutorials
- Quantum Country - Free Book on Quantum Computing

Conclusion: The Future is Yours to Shape

In this final section, we emphasize that while the future job market may seem uncertain, those who are proactive, adaptable, and continuously learning will be well-positioned to succeed. It's important to approach your career with a growth mindset, embrace change, and stay informed about emerging trends. With the right preparation, the future offers limitless opportunities for those who are ready to seize them.

Chapter 26: Embracing the Future with Confidence

Introduction

As we close this book, it's important to reflect on everything we've discussed. The future of jobs may seem uncertain, and with emerging technologies like AI and automation, it's natural to feel overwhelmed or even fearful. But throughout history, we've faced similar moments of change, and each time, humanity has not only adapted but thrived. This chapter is meant to offer hope and motivation, helping you see that the future holds immense potential, not just challenges.

A Lesson from History: Opportunities in Every Revolution

Whenever there has been significant technological change, people have felt afraid of losing their livelihoods. Let's take the **Industrial Revolution** as an example. When machines began automating processes in factories, there was widespread fear that humans would be replaced. But what happened? Instead of erasing jobs, the Industrial Revolution opened up countless new opportunities. New industries emerged, and millions of jobs were created, from factory workers to engineers, entrepreneurs, and innovators. The world saw a surge in economic growth and a higher standard of living.

The same thing happened when **computers** began to revolutionize the workplace. People feared that automation and digital systems would make human workers obsolete. But instead, computers created entire industries, software development, IT, digital marketing, and many more. Today, millions of jobs exist that didn't even have names a few decades ago.

As we move into a future shaped by AI, automation, and technology, the key takeaway is this: **new opportunities will always emerge**. Change brings challenges, but it also brings growth. What's different this time is that **soft skills**, things like creativity, emotional intelligence, critical thinking, and collaboration, will become more valuable than ever. While machines handle the hard, technical tasks, humans will focus on innovation, strategy, and development. The future will be about **thinking, not doing**.

Jobs Will Evolve, Not Disappear

As we've seen with past revolutions, jobs don't disappear, they evolve. In the future, you may not need to be an expert in technical skills like coding or machine operation because AI will handle much of that. Instead, your value will come from your ability to imagine new possibilities, create strategies, and collaborate with others.

Think of yourself not as someone competing with machines, but as someone **working alongside** them. You will be able to focus on

what machines cannot do: lead teams, empathize with customers, develop innovative ideas, and shape the future of industries.

So, while the technical landscape may change, the **core human qualities** that have always been valuable, **curiosity, creativity, and empathy**, will remain essential.

Motivational Sayings to Keep in Mind

To further inspire you, let's reflect on some wisdom from great thinkers and leaders. These quotes remind us of the importance of staying resilient and hopeful, even in uncertain times.

1. **"Instead of cursing the darkness, light a candle."**
   This famous saying, often attributed to Confucius and later popularized by Eleanor Roosevelt, reminds us that when faced with challenges, we have a choice: we can either complain about the difficulties or take action and create solutions.
2. **"The only thing we have to fear is fear itself."**
   , Franklin D. Roosevelt
   This quote encourages us to face the future with courage, understanding that fear can often be a barrier to progress. The best way forward is to embrace the opportunities that change brings.

3. **"The best way to predict the future is to create it."**
   , Peter Drucker

   This saying reflects the importance of taking control of your own destiny. Instead of worrying about what will happen, focus on building the future you want.

4. **"Do not wait for leaders; do it alone, person to person."**
   , Mother Teresa

   This reminds us that we have the power to make changes ourselves. The future of jobs won't be shaped only by governments or corporations; it will be shaped by individuals like you taking initiative.

5. **"In the middle of difficulty lies opportunity."**
   , Albert Einstein

   Every challenge you face is an opportunity in disguise. The future may present difficulties, but those who see beyond the obstacles will find the most success.

Hope for the Future: Soft Skills Are the Key

You might be wondering: with so many technical advancements, where do humans fit in? The answer is simple, **soft skills**. Soft skills are uniquely human. Machines can analyze data and perform tasks, but they cannot think creatively, solve complex problems with nuance, or navigate human emotions. The future of work will prioritize these human-centric skills, which means that **everyone** can contribute meaningfully, regardless of technical expertise.

Think of your role in the future as a **creator and innovator**. Machines will handle the mundane, freeing you to think about big ideas, develop strategies, and build relationships.

Taking Action: Light Your Candle

The famous quote, "Instead of cursing the darkness, light a candle," teaches us an important lesson: sitting back and worrying about the future will not bring positive change. Action does. Instead of fearing what the future holds, take steps today to **shape your future**. Whether it's learning a new skill, starting a new project, or simply thinking about how you can bring value to the world, now is the time to start.

The future isn't something to fear; it's something to build. Remember that every generation has faced its own challenges, but through action and innovation, they overcame them and created a better world. You have the same potential.

Conclusion

As you close this book, know that the future is not something to be afraid of, but something to embrace. Yes, jobs will change, but new ones will emerge, ones that are more meaningful, creative, and impactful than ever before. The skills that truly matter, **your ability to think, to innovate, to connect with others**, will always be in demand. So, instead of worrying, start preparing. The future is yours to shape.

References:

- Confucius (Attributed). "Instead of cursing the darkness, light a candle."
- F.D. Roosevelt, Inaugural Address, 1933.
- Peter Drucker, *Management Challenges for the 21st Century*, 1999.
- Albert Einstein, *Einstein: His Life and Universe*, Walter Isaacson, 2007.
- Mother Teresa, Nobel Peace Prize Speech, 1979.

www.ingramcontent.com/pod-product-compliance
Lightning Source LLC
Chambersburg PA
CBHW031624210526
45464CB00004B/1734